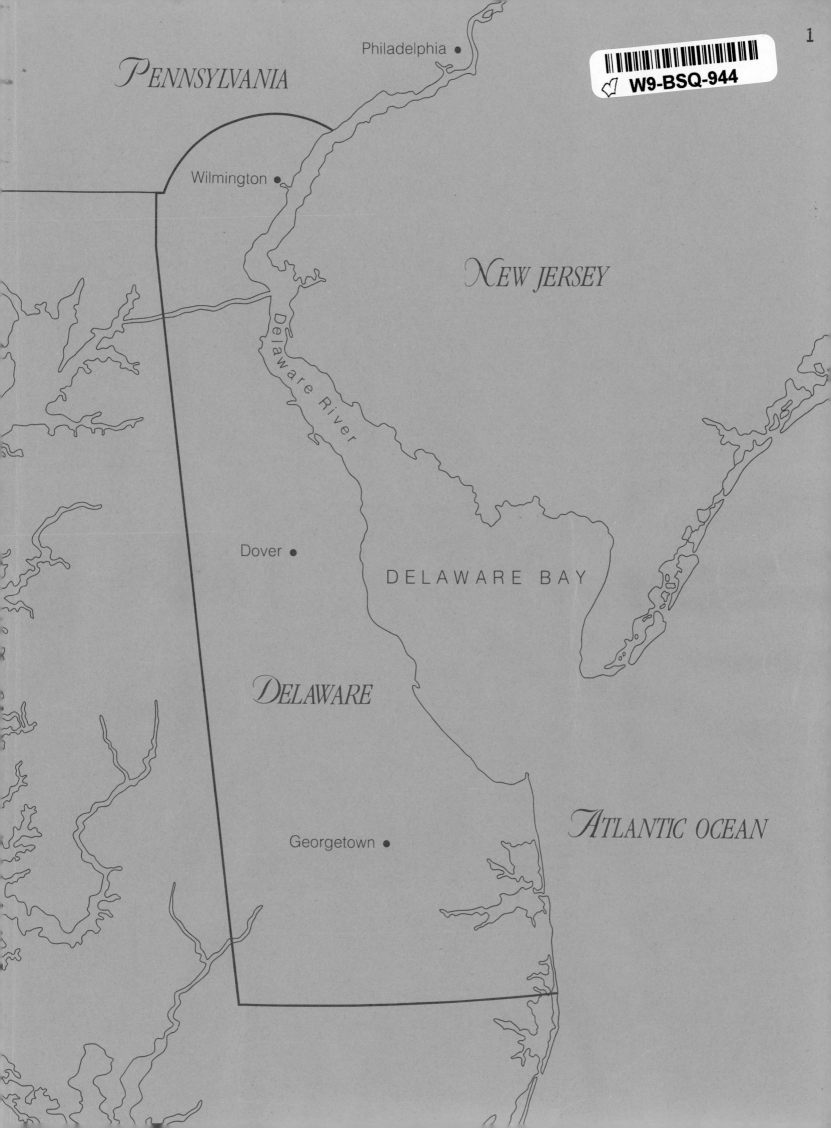

PENNSYLVANIA

Philadelphia •

Wilmington •

NEW JERSEY

Delaware River

Dover •

DELAWARE BAY

DELAWARE

Georgetown •

ATLANTIC OCEAN

DELAWARE
SMALL WONDER

DELAWARE

SMALL WONDER

PHOTOGRAPHS BY KEVIN FLEMING
INTRODUCTION BY CAROL E. HOFFECKER
TEXT BY JANE VESSELS
MAPS BY MARLEY AMSTUTZ

Library of Congress Cataloging in Publication
Fleming, Kevin.
Delaware, small wonder.
Bibliography: p.
Includes index.
1. Delaware—Description and travel—1981—
Views.
2. Delaware—History—Pictorial works.
I. Vessels, Jane. II. Title.
F165.F57 1984 975.1 84-2836
ISBN 0-8109-0826-3
ISBN 0-8109-2285-1 (pbk.)

PUBLISHED BY THE
STATE OF DELAWARE AND

HARRY N. ABRAMS, INC.,
PUBLISHERS, NEW YORK

Editor: Darlene Geis
Designer: Bob McKee

Printed and bound in Japan

CONTENTS

The cupola of Legislative Hall in Dover.

DEDICATION

Dedications usually bring fanfare—cornerstones are cemented, champagne bottles broken, shiny shovels scratch the earth, and streamers are cut with large carpet shears. During my service with the State, I have been privileged to attend many of these events —for hotels and hospitals, warehouses and workshops, banks, barges, bridges, and baseball fields. Each event has highlighted a new project that will improve the living or working conditions of a specific group and indirectly enrich the general welfare of all.

Happily, now I have the opportunity to offer a quieter note of gratitude to you, the people of Delaware, who have made the dedication of this book a reality. You provide the enormous diversity of background and life-style that has given inspiration to Kevin Fleming and his camera. Your warmth and dogged independence go back more than three hundred fifty years, as Carol Hoffecker and Jane Vessels have so clearly documented. Your history and culture are preserved in many locations, identified on the maps drawn by Marley Amstutz. Your elected representatives have provided the public support necessary to help this book reach your living room, office, or library. Your business, educational, cultural, and political accomplishments will continue to bring new ideas and events to Delaware, perhaps to be recorded in some future edition of this book. Finally, your collective determination to balance economic growth with conservation has preserved much of the beauty recorded on these pages. I hope that you will enjoy the results of our work as much as we have enjoyed the hours invested in its preparation. You have made Delaware truly "the Small Wonder," and with many thanks, this book is dedicated to you.

Nathan Hayward III
Director, Delaware Development Office

INTRODUCTION

COLONIZATION TO STATEHOOD

For a state smaller than Yellowstone National Park and with fewer people than three New York City Council districts, Delaware has had a remarkable impact on the history, culture, and business growth not only of the Mid-Atlantic region but of our entire nation.

It was the first state to join the Union, yet few people outside the surrounding area seem aware of its existence. It is the only state that is neither north nor south of the Mason-Dixon line. It is predominantly rural and agricultural, yet it is also the legal home of more than half the Fortune 500 companies and the headquarters of a number of America's industrial giants. Although it straddles the populous Washington–New York belt, its quiet farms and tidal marshes seem centuries removed from the high-speed pace of the Amtrak corridor. In short, Delaware is an anomaly within East Coast USA.

Historically the state has been defined by the bay and river from which it takes its name. Delaware's three counties lie along the eastern side of the Delmarva Peninsula, the flat sandy neck of land that separates the Chesapeake and Delaware bays. In the seventeenth century, when the nations of Western Europe were jockeying for empires in the New World, the river—which the Dutch explorer Henry Hudson called the South River and the English called the Delaware—provided an avenue to inland bounty. The native Americans who inhabited the banks of the big river and its many tributaries were a peaceful people and poorly organized to thwart the materialistic designs of European newcomers. At first valued by their discoverers because they could supply pelts for the lucrative fur trade, the Indians were later harassed and driven from their homelands. Only a few Nanticoke Indian descendants remain in Delaware, and most can be found close to the river that bears their name. It is the one Delaware watershed that drains westward through Maryland to the Chesapeake Bay.

Delaware's birth was scarred by colonial infighting unparalleled in the history of any of the other original settlements. In 1631, two decades after Henry Hudson had discovered the Delaware Bay and River, the Dutch established a fishing settlement named Zwannendael, or Valley of Swans, just beyond the sand dunes inside Cape Henlopen on the site of present-day Lewes. A misunderstanding between the Dutchmen in this tiny outpost and their Indian neighbors led to the untimely destruction of the village.

In 1638 Sweden planted the first permanent settlement in the Delaware River Valley at the mouth of the Christina River. The Swedes had recently emerged as a major European power under the leadership of their soldier-king Gustavus Adolphus. The King saw colonization as a means to greater national wealth and glory, but unfortunately he was killed in a battle while preparations for the colonial effort were in progress. His young daughter, Christina, could not maintain her father's expansionist policies and gave the colony of New Sweden anemic support by sending only a few boatloads of Swedish and Finnish farmers and artisans to the colony. The settlers were accustomed to big forests and frontier conditions at home and managed to eke out a living in the New World, but they could not make the colony profitable. Probably their most significant contribution was their introduction of the log cabin into the New World.

The Dutch, who regarded the Swedes as interlopers in the river valley's fur trade, never acknowledged the little colony's right to exist and conquered it with ease in 1655. The commercially minded Dutch then established a little hamlet called New Amstel, the first town on the Delaware River. This modest settlement, (later renamed New Castle), the fishing village at Lewes, and a rural village on the St. Jones River midway between the two became focal points for the creation of Delaware's three counties—later named by the English New Castle, Kent, and Sussex. Each instituted its own county court to administer the affairs of the settlers, a system of governance which survives today in the Levy Court of Kent, home of Delaware's capital city of Dover. The three counties soon became known as New Netherland.

During these three decades the English had established populous, productive roots north of New Netherland in New England and south in the tobacco colonies of the Chesapeake tidewater. When conflict between England and Holland erupted into war in 1664, an English fleet commanded by James, Duke of York, brother of King Charles II, seized New Amsterdam and all of New Netherland, claiming these territories for the British sovereign.

From the mid-1660's until the Revolution, the lands along the west bank of the Delaware River were ruled by Englishmen, first by the Duke of York and later by William Penn and his heirs. During this century the very existence of Delaware as a colony was in doubt. The Penns of Pennsylvania and the Calverts of Maryland fought a lengthy legal battle for the right to incorporate Sussex, the southernmost county in Delaware, into their other proprietary lands. Had the Marylanders won, New Castle and Kent would probably have been insufficient to constitute a separate entity and the remaining part of colonial Delaware would have been absorbed into Pennsylvania. While the case was being heard before the English court, the Calverts made large grants of property in southern Delaware to Marylanders loyal to them. These men brought their slaves and other features of the Chesapeake tidewater way of life to Delaware. The controversy over land ownership was finally resolved in the Penn family's favor, and in 1763 the English court hired two young surveyors, Charles Mason and Jeremiah Dixon, to mark the boundaries between the

proprietors' disputed territory. The Mason-Dixon line is really two lines, running east–west to separate Maryland from Pennsylvania, and north–south dividing present-day Maryland from Delaware. Long after statehood, little Delaware was still fighting for every inch of territory it could claim, and it took a 1934 U.S. Supreme Court decision to establish once and for all the line between Delaware and New Jersey, which now runs in the Delaware River, to mean low water on New Jersey's western shore, and then jogs south along the historic thalweg or ship channel to the mouth of the Bay.

While southern and western Delaware were heavily influenced by Maryland, the northern and eastern portions of New Castle County were developing in harmony with their nearest neighbor, Pennsylvania. Shortly after Charles II granted the province of Pennsylvania to William Penn in 1682, the King's brother, James, gave the Quaker leader a long-term lease on his Delaware territories, then called the "Three Lower Counties on Delaware." Penn planned to incorporate his province and his territories into a single administrative unit with a single governor and a legislature that would fairly represent all of the resident colonists. His hopes for amalgamation were dashed, however, because the Swedes, Finns, Dutch, English, and Africans who lived in the three lower counties were continually at odds with the more homogeneous English Quakers who populated Pennsylvania. Finally, in 1701, Penn reluctantly acceded to the demands of his legislators and permitted the Delawareans a separate legislative body. By this act and by his subsequent victory over Calvert in their contest for territory, Penn guaranteed the autonomy of what was to become the nation's first state.

In spite of ethnic, religious, and political differences, Quaker Pennsylvania exercised considerable influence over the lower counties. Most important, the Quakers' commercial center of Philadelphia shaped the economy of the whole Delaware River basin. Quaker merchants led the development of market-oriented agriculture, especially the production of wheat. Colonial Philadelphia grew rapidly on its thriving grain trade and inspired the creation of other towns, carrying commerce deeper into the hinterland. One of these towns was Wilmington, founded by Quaker merchants and millers in the 1730's near the site of the old Swedish colony at the confluence of the Christina, Brandywine, and Delaware rivers.

The invention of new flour milling machinery in 1785 helped spur Wilmington's growth as a commercial town famous for its Brandywine superfine flour. But geography played a large role in this prosperity and underscores the major topographical division between the three counties. The area north and west of Wilmington is part of the piedmont plateau's rolling hills and rapidly flowing streams. This region, lying astride the fall line that runs from Philadelphia to Baltimore, was well adapted to waterpowered industries. In contrast, the flat coastal plain of the peninsula, with its slow, meandering rivers, accounts for nine-tenths of Delaware's roughly 2,000 square miles. Thus, even before the Revolutionary War, Delaware's social, economic, and political patterns were evolving into an upstate-downstate dichotomy based upon geographical features.

The political crisis that produced the American Revolution brought special challenges to such a small state. When all thirteen colonies threw off the yoke of British domination, Delaware's statesmen renounced allegiance not only to Great Britain, but to Pennsylvania as well. The state's constitution of 1776 proclaimed that the Three Lower Counties on Delaware were henceforth to be called the Delaware State. In casting his famous tie-breaking vote for national independence, after an all-night ride to Philadelphia from Dover, Caesar Rodney made certain that Delaware would remain as independent as any of her sister states. Although the little state was forced to rely on outsiders, clearly Delaware's best interests lay in the creation of a national government that would acknowledge the independence of the states, but would also prevent big states from taking unfair advantage of their smaller neighbors. When the Constitutional Convention in Philadelphia produced a document that promised just such a balance, Delawareans moved so quickly to ratify the new Constitution that they gained the honor of becoming the first state to enter the Union, on December 7, 1787.

THE INDUSTRIAL REVOLUTION AND CIVIL WAR

The Civil War erupted from a growing division between the country's industrializing North and slave-holding, agrarian South. The differences that nearly destroyed a great nation were strongly felt in Delaware. Upstate in New Castle County, Wilmington had become an industrial center that attracted immigrants from Ireland, Germany, and England to work in its foundries, tanneries, and carriage-making shops. A Wilmington firm produced the first iron-hulled ship built in America, and the city was a center for railroad car manufacture. Nearby along the Brandywine were located grist, paper, and textile mills. J. E. Rhoads & Sons, maker of leather industrial belts, was established in Wilmington to supply the millers' needs, and it now claims prominence as the nation's oldest surviving company, having operated constantly since its founding in 1702. The Brandywine's excellent qualities for generating waterpower also attracted the French emigré Eleuthère Irénée du Pont, who in 1802 established a black powder mill two miles north of Wilmington that was the seed from which the largest chemical company in America eventually grew.

While northern Delaware shared in the industrial growth of the northeastern United States, most of the First State remained rural and retained the slave system inherited from colonial times. Delaware's farmers did not produce staples such as cotton or sugar as did the big plantation owners of the South. Most farmers in Delaware engaged in general farming, raising various grains, hogs, and some dairy cattle. Large landowners employed tenant farmers or used slaves to work their land.

Improvements in transportation during the nineteenth century had the greatest impact on farming in Delaware. Steamboats built in Wilmington and Philadelphia appeared on the Delaware River early in the century and made scheduled calls at wharfs along its tributaries to pick up passengers and farm produce. In the 1820's a canal was dug across southern New Castle County to link the Chesapeake Bay to the Delaware River. Designed to assist the flow of trade between Philadelphia and Baltimore, the canal brought Delaware farmers closer to urban markets. Major Philip Reybold, son of a Philadelphia sheep-dresser, was most successful in seizing this opportunity. From his farms along the banks of the canal at Delaware City, Reybold shipped butter to Baltimore and peaches to Philadelphia. His orchards were so productive that he soon became known as "The Peach King." At harvest time every steamship on the Delaware hastened to Reybold's wharf to load buckets of the juicy, highly perishable fruit and speed them to Philadelphia and New York.

Few Delaware farmers could join in this peach bonanza until the 1850's, when the Delaware Railroad was constructed from Wilmington downstate to Seaford on the Nanticoke River. The rails made the southern and western portions of the state easily accessible for the first time, and new towns, villages, and peach orchards sprang up along the line. Canneries appeared in every town, and successful producers and canners built mansion houses curlicued with the gingerbread decoration so dear to the Victorian heart. But the bonanza was short-lived. A disease called "the yellows" attacked the state's orchards, spreading south from Delaware City and destroying the young fruit trees in its all-embracing wake. By the century's end Major Reybold's orchards had lost their 10,000 trees and farmers elsewhere on the peninsula reverted to raising grain and vegetables.

As a border state neither above nor below the Mason-Dixon line, Delaware has had a history long marked by deeply conflicting views concerning race. Slavery, although still legal, was rapidly dying out in Delaware when Abraham Lincoln was elected President in 1860. Lincoln's inauguration was greeted with little joy in Delaware except among the Republican merchants and industrialists of Wilmington. There was an active underground railroad in the state organized by the gallant Marylander and former slave Harriet Tubman and an equally resolute Wilmington Quaker merchant named Thomas Garrett. But judging from election results and politicians' oratory, most of the state's voters approved of slavery, or at least were unwilling to oppose it. Delawareans drew the line at secession, however.

When representatives of newly seceded states from the Deep South urged the Delaware General Assembly to join the Confederacy, they were told that the first state to adopt our country's Constitution would be the last to abandon it.

No Civil War battles were fought in Delaware, but the state was nonetheless seriously affected by the war. Men from the First State fought on opposite sides, while towns and even families were split by conflicting loyalties. Thousands of Confederate prisoners of war were confined within the gray stone walls of Fort Delaware on marshy Pea Patch Island in the Delaware River, and Union soldiers diligently guarded the Du Pont powder works, which supplied vital munitions to the northern army.

Slavery ended in Delaware with the adoption of the 13th Amendment in 1865. Before that date, the state's free blacks had established a strong sense of community spirit, nurtured by religious organizations. Itinerant Methodist preachers had long been influential on the Delaware Peninsula. Early in the history of the faith, black Methodists created their own interstate African Methodist Union, which held its annual religious and social celebration called Big Quarterly, at the Mother Church in Wilmington. But the outcome of the Civil War did not bring profound changes to the lives of black Delawareans. Politicians who opposed black suffrage found legal subterfuges to keep blacks from the polls. The state government reluctantly created a segregated school system for blacks but provided so little funding that most of the schools were little more than ramshackle hovels.

DELAWARE IN THE TWENTIETH CENTURY

Big changes came to Delaware in the first decades of the twentieth century. In 1902 three energetic young men, T. Coleman, Pierre S., and Alfred I. du Pont, took control of the Du Pont Company, and the du Pont cousins began turning their family inheritance into an efficient, aggressive "Big Business" organization. They also left an indelible mark on their native state. T. Coleman du Pont was an engineer intrigued by money, politics, and the potential of the motor car. In 1911 he astonished the state legislature when he proposed building a four-lane highway the entire length of Delaware which he would give to the state. Skeptics were sure that the millionaire businessman possessed some secret scheme to make money on the venture, but du Pont, without personal profit and at a cost of $40,000,000, constructed what was then the most modern highway in the country. It is hard to exaggerate the importance of his gift to the state. The du Pont Highway became the spine on which subsequent roads could be grafted and the means of generating new prosperity for Delaware's southern farms and northern industries.

Pierre S. du Pont's benefactions to education in Delaware were even more generous and significant. During the 1920's he personally underwrote the cost of constructing modern consolidated schools for both white and black students throughout the state, and as state treasurer he remodeled Delaware's taxes to ensure that the school system would have a steady flow of income. With his help the state perfected its model corporation law, which has attracted thousands of out-of-state businesses to Delaware and has earned the state an unequaled reputation as a home for corporate administration.

Through the efforts of Alfred I. du Pont, the state's shamefully archaic almshouses were replaced by a single well-equipped welfare home. His legacy includes the Nemours Foundation, which finances the A. I. du Pont Institute, one of the world's leading orthopedic hospitals, and a variety of health care programs for the state's medically needy elderly population. Thanks to the early leadership of these men, Delaware's conservative-minded state government eventually accepted responsibility for maintaining a high level of publicly financed service, particularly in public education.

In the course of the twentieth century, the du Ponts and their company have wrought other dramatic changes in Delaware. Under Pierre's leadership, the Du Pont Company enlarged its production far beyond explosives to encompass a variety of highly technical chemical commodities such as paint pigments, rayon, cellophane,

and that most lucrative discovery yet to come from a Du Pont laboratory, nylon. As Du Pont grew, so did Delaware. In 1906 the company began construction of a large combination office building, theater, and hotel in the heart of downtown Wilmington. In the midst of that project, the federal government brought an antitrust suit against the company that led to the creation of two new powder companies, Hercules and Atlas. Each established its corporate headquarters in Wilmington and, like Du Pont, moved into the production of chemical products—prompting Wilmingtonians to call their city the "chemical capital of the world." Management, research, and development in this highly technical industry changed the shape of Wilmington's economy in the years after the First World War. The city's older industries —leather, shipbuilding, and milling—became less prominent. Comfortable suburbs were constructed adjacent to the city, and in the rolling piedmont north and west of Wilmington, which Delawareans now call "chateau country," the farmlands were transformed into estates. Nor was downstate Delaware neglected. In the late 1930's Du Pont chose Seaford as the site for its first nylon plant. This complex on the banks of the Nanticoke River remains the largest production center for nylon in the country.

In the years after World War II, the region between Washington and New York has grown into one giant megalopolis, but Delawareans have successfully managed to temper continued development with traditional rural tranquility. The millions of trucks and cars that travel Interstate 95 en route between New York and Washington seem a world away from the flat salt marshes of Bombay Hook National Wildlife Refuge, only 30 miles south on the Delaware Bay, where great flocks of migrating birds stop off on their semiannual journeys. The state's pioneering Coastal Zone Act, adopted in 1971, has helped maintain the state's wetlands and the delicate ecological balance so essential for both fish and fowl. Delaware was one of the first states to adopt tough environmental laws, and its citizens jealously guard their parklands and open spaces. Quality of life in Delaware has always been a major consideration for corporate and political leaders, and an equilibrium between growth and conservation seems firmly rooted throughout the state.

Delaware's agricultural land continues to be among the country's most productive, and excellent proximity to urban markets guarantees a bright future for this industry. The eighteenth-century river trade in wheat and the nineteenth-century railroad trade in peaches have given way to a new means of locomotion and production. Today Delaware produces more than 180 million broiler chickens per year, which supply the fast-food franchises and supermarkets of the northeastern United States. Corn and soybeans are grown throughout the state to feed the young birds, which are carried to market by fleets of trucks that traverse Delaware's highways every day.

Modern Delaware possesses a remarkably balanced economy for such a small state. Since 1960 the downstate counties have been gaining population faster than urban, industrial New Castle in the north. In addition to chickens and nylon, Sussex County has burgeoning resort and retirement communities along her beautiful Atlantic beaches and saltwater bays. In recent years the quaint seaside town of Rehoboth, whose big old clapboard country houses once offered a tranquil summer retreat, has become a major east coast recreational playground. So many hot-weather transplants come from Washington that the area has become known as the "Nation's Summer Capital." Kent County, known for its agriculture and food processing industries, is also the home of Dover Air Force Base, where giant C-5 cargo planes ferry material across the Atlantic to Europe and beyond. In New Castle County and its economic hub, Wilmington, out-of-state banking operations have recently joined the chemical companies and the law firms that form the corporate underpinnings of the region's highly professional white-collar economy. In nearby Newark, the University of Delaware has become a significant element in the state's economic future with its sea grant research and pioneering work in chemical engineering. Automobile production at two of the country's most modern plants employs more than three percent of Delaware's work force. Retailing throughout the state is spurred by the absence of any state sales tax, and cars from many surrounding states routinely fill the parking lots of Delaware's shopping centers.

In the midst of the rapid changes associated with these developments, little Delaware proudly clings to its less hurried traditions. When the ocean beaches of Sussex are crowded on a summer's day, one can still find quiet relaxation by boating on the state's inland lakes, visiting the northernmost bald cypress swamp in America, or touring some of the country's finest museums in the rural setting of the Brandywine Valley. Below the droning Air Force transports and beyond the commercial strip development of Route 13, the state buildings on Dover's old town green display a dignity, simplicity, and charm unusual for a state capital. And upstate in the historic town of New Castle, time seems little changed from the early nineteenth century when prosperous lawyers built handsome brick residences around its courthouse square.

Delaware is truly unpretentious—while it is a state old in tradition it is still young in possibilities. It is a place that newcomers quickly learn to enjoy and cherish. Personal associations are very important in this small state where citizens consider face-to-face meetings with business and political leaders routine, and where the daily affairs of commerce and government are conducted on a first-name basis. Its location on the Delmarva Peninsula has protected its privacy without sacrificing the advantages of close contact with the nearby bustling eastern corridor. Delaware is a state that offers the natural beauty of tidal marshes and ocean beaches as well as the man-made beauty of furniture and fine arts collections. Its citizens exhibit a predilection for simplicity and quiet living even as its growing business community breaks new ground in chemicals, medicines, and finance.

Although the fascinating diversity of this little state may come as a surprise to many of its outside visitors, to its longtime residents it is an accepted fact that Delaware is truly "the Small Wonder."

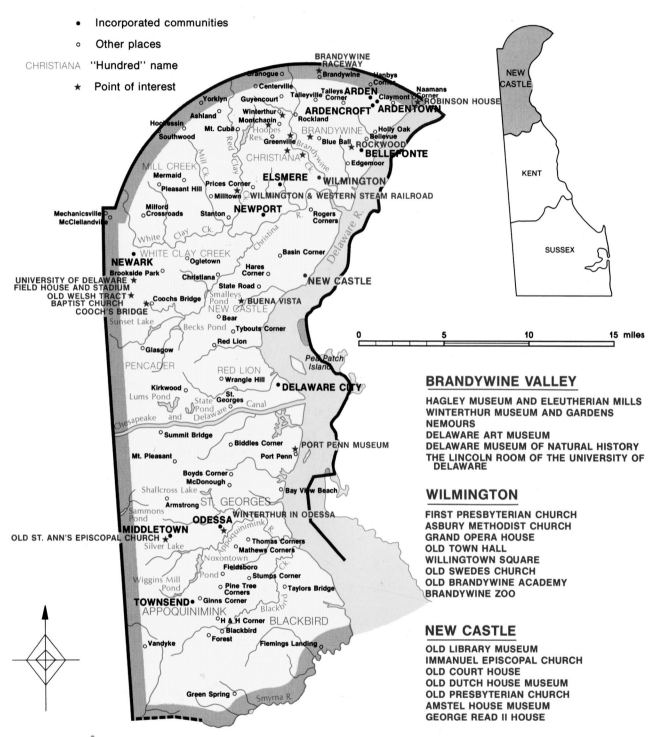

- • Incorporated communities
- ○ Other places

CHRISTIANA "Hundred" name

★ Point of interest

BRANDYWINE
RACEWAY

Granogue

○ Centerville

Brandywine ★

Hanbys
Corner

Naamans
Corner

Yorklyn

Guyencourt

Talleyville
Corner

Talleys
Corner

ARDEN

Claymont

ROBINSON HOUSE ★

Winterthur ○

Ashland

ARDENCROFT

ARDENTOWN

Hockessin

Montchanin ○

Rockland

Mt. Cuba ○

Hoopes
Res.

BRANDYWINE

Holly Oak

Southwood

Greenville ★

Blue Ball

Bellevue

MILL CREEK

Mermaid

CHRISTIANA

ROCKWOOD ★

Edgemoor ○

BELLEFONTE

Prices Corner ○

ELSMERE

★ WILMINGTON

Pleasant Hill ○

Milltown ○

WILMINGTON & WESTERN STEAM RAILROAD

Milford
Crossroads ○

Stanton ○

NEWPORT

Rogers
Corners ○

Mechanicsville ●
McClellandville ●

White   Clay   Ck.

WHITE CLAY CREEK

Ogletown ○

Basin Corner ○

NEWARK

Brookside Park ○

Christiana ○

Hares
Corner ○

UNIVERSITY OF DELAWARE ★
FIELD HOUSE AND STADIUM
OLD WELSH TRACT ★
BAPTIST CHURCH
COOCH'S BRIDGE

Coochs Bridge ○

State Road ○

NEW CASTLE

Smalleys
Pond

★ BUENA VISTA

NEW CASTLE

Bear ○

Sunset Lake

Becks Pond

Tybouts Corner ○

Red Lion ○

Glasgow ○

PENCADER

RED LION

Pea Patch
Island

Wrangle Hill ○

Kirkwood ○

DELAWARE CITY

Lums Pond

St.
Georges ○

State
Pond
Delaware

Canal

Chesapeake   and

Summit Bridge ○

Biddles Corner ○

PORT PENN MUSEUM

Mt. Pleasant ○

Port Penn ○

Boyds Corner ○
McDonough ○

Shallcross Lake

Bay View Beach ○

Sammons
Pond

Armstrong ○

ST. GEORGES

ODESSA ●

WINTERTHUR IN ODESSA

OLD ST. ANN'S EPISCOPAL CHURCH ★

MIDDLETOWN ●

Silver Lake

Appoquinimink R.

Thomas Corners ○

Mathews Corners ○

Noxontown
Pond

Fieldsboro ○

Wiggins Mill
Pond

Pine Tree
Corners ○

Stumps Corner ○

Taylors Bridge ○

TOWNSEND ●

Ginns Corner ○

APPOQUINIMINK

Blackbird Ck.

H & H Corner ○

BLACKBIRD

Vandyke ○

Blackbird ○

Forest ○

Flemings Landing ○

Green Spring ○

Smyrna R.

NEW
CASTLE

KENT

SUSSEX

0   5   10   15 miles

BRANDYWINE VALLEY

HAGLEY MUSEUM AND ELEUTHERIAN MILLS
WINTERTHUR MUSEUM AND GARDENS
NEMOURS
DELAWARE ART MUSEUM
DELAWARE MUSEUM OF NATURAL HISTORY
THE LINCOLN ROOM OF THE UNIVERSITY OF
    DELAWARE

WILMINGTON

FIRST PRESBYTERIAN CHURCH
ASBURY METHODIST CHURCH
GRAND OPERA HOUSE
OLD TOWN HALL
WILLINGTOWN SQUARE
OLD SWEDES CHURCH
OLD BRANDYWINE ACADEMY
BRANDYWINE ZOO

NEW CASTLE

OLD LIBRARY MUSEUM
IMMANUEL EPISCOPAL CHURCH
OLD COURT HOUSE
OLD DUTCH HOUSE MUSEUM
OLD PRESBYTERIAN CHURCH
AMSTEL HOUSE MUSEUM
GEORGE READ II HOUSE

Communities with several points of interest are identified by color and a list is provided in the margin

NEW CASTLE

Smallest but most populous of Delaware's three counties, New Castle is home to two-thirds of the state's 602,000 residents. Most live in or around Wilmington, the state's largest city, and Newark, home of the University of Delaware.

But a rural flavor prevails in the southern half of New Castle County below the Chesapeake and Delaware Canal. Much of the land is farmed, and whispering coastal marshes support migratory waterfowl and a large population of muskrats, trapped during the winter for their fur and savory meat.

Above the Chesapeake and Delaware Canal lie Delaware's heaviest industries—rail and maritime commerce, an oil refinery, automobile assembly plants, and chemical research and manufacturing led by Du Pont, Hercules, and ICI Americas. Here, too, the geography changes as the piedmont plateau rises from the coastal plain. In the northwest crescent above Wilmington, urban landscapes give way to sheltering woods and the rolling grounds of country estates in the Brandywine Valley.

The state's distinctive northern border—an arc with a twelve-mile radius measured from the courthouse in the town of New Castle—was devised in 1681 to separate the colonies on the Delaware River from William Penn's Pennsylvania. The following year Penn was also granted the remainder of the land that is today Delaware, and made his first New World stop in New Castle to claim it.

A passion for steam fuels the all-volunteer Wilmington and Western Railroad as it runs historical excursions through the Red Clay Valley and here in the Brandywine Valley, where the sights include Granogue. a 515-acre du Pont estate built in 1923.

A triumph of cast-iron-façade architecture, Wilmington's Grand Opera House was built by the Masons in 1871. Restored in 1976 as Delaware's Center for the Performing Arts, it hosts the Delaware Symphony, Opera Delaware, and the Delaware Ballet, as well as local and nationally touring artists.

Signer of the Declaration of Independence, Caesar Rodney gallops in bronze overlooking Wilmington's Rodney Square to commemorate his July 1776 dash from Dover to the Second Continental Congress in Philadelphia. Delaware's delegates were divided until Rodney rode all night to swing Delaware's vote to independence, allowing the colonies to present a united front against Great Britain.

A Wilmington building boom means booming business for brother and sister window washers Butch and Wendy Campbell, hoisted across from Rodney Square and the twelve-story Du Pont Building. The Du Pont Company launched the city's reputation as the Chemical Capital in 1902 when it moved headquarters downtown and completed this office in 1912. The building expanded the next year to create the Playhouse Theater and the Hotel du Pont—graced by original paintings from the Brandywine School of Art and famed for its cuisine.

A bold statement in granite and glass, the new world headquarters of Hercules Incorporated dominates the Brandywine Gateway, a Wilmington redevelopment project spawning new offices, restaurants, parks, and housing. As additional city and state incentives lure companies to build in corresponding Christina Gateway, the downtown revival spreads from river to river.

Morning light gilds Du Pont Company offices, which now span three blocks and also include the headquarters of Conoco, acquired by Du Pont in 1981. Nearby, shadows cross a courtyard beside a new complex housing Wilmington, New Castle County, and state government offices.

Wilmington's early history can be traced among the tombstones in the graveyard that surrounds and predates Old Swedes Church (right), one of the oldest churches still used for worship in North America.

It was built as Trinity Church in 1698 by the descendants of Swedish settlers who sixty years earlier established a community on the Christina River.

Wilmington's skyline is growing more complex as this leading center for the chemical industry and corporate law has begun to attract financial institutions. The 1981 Financial Center Development Act invites out-of-state banks to operate in Delaware, offering them tax incentives, lower operating costs, and a locale free of interest-rate ceilings. More than a dozen banks, including J. P. Morgan, Chase Manhattan, and Citicorp have opened Delaware subsidiaries.

A street-wise quarterback foils his taggers in east Wilmington near Old Swedes Church. Artistic energies flow in the former parish house of Old Swedes, now the Christina Cultural Arts Center, dedicated to providing inexpensive training in music, dance, painting, and drama, and promoting black culture. Today more than 50 percent black, Wilmington in the 19th century was an important station on the Underground Railroad, when the city's Quakers assisted fleeing slaves.

The state's busiest traffic corridor, and one of its highest elevations, the Delaware Memorial Bridge peaks 441 feet above the Delaware River. Ferries shuttled between Delaware and New Jersey until the first span opened just south of Wilmington in 1951. A twin span now carrying traffic toward the lights of Delaware rose in 1968.

Peaceful at daybreak, this key crossroads of mid-Atlantic traffic joins Delaware's major north-south highway, Route 13, with the underpassing Interstate 295, a spur that links the New Jersey Turnpike with Interstate 95 via the Delaware Memorial Bridge. Each year more than 33 million vehicles pass through toll plazas on the bridge and at the Maryland-Delaware line, making this 13-mile stretch of highway one of the busiest in the country.

A major switching yard on the mainline of Conrail, Wilmington's Edgemoor Transportation Center annually handles millions of dollars of freight. Tracks link it to the Chessie System's Railroads in nearby Elsmere, the Northeast headquarters for Chessie's piggyback freight. Another major rail center is the Amtrak Northeast repair yard located in Wilmington. In the 1870s, the city led the nation in railroad-car building and shipped cars as far as London, Paris, and China.

A multimillion-dollar facelift renews Wilmington's passenger train station as part of a federal effort to upgrade Amtrak's Northeast Corridor. Terra-cotta window arches and a red-clay tile roof accent the unusual eclectic architecture of the station, in service since 1905 and now on the National Register of Historic Places.

Drawing on the power of Brandywine Creek and his expert training in chemistry, French immigrant Eleuthère Irénée du Pont launched a business empire north of Wilmington in 1802. By mid-century, E. I. Du Pont de Nemours and Company was the nation's largest gunpowder producer. Forty percent of the explosives supplied to World War I Allied Forces came from Du Pont plants. The original Hagley Mills operated until 1921, when a diversified Du Pont was well on its way to becoming the largest chemical company in the U.S. Black powder subsequently gave way to such revolutionary inventions as nylon, Dacron, and Teflon.

The original powder yards and the mill workers' community are now preserved as the Hagley Museum. Working displays illustrate many facets of early American industries and the Hagley Library does modern duty as an archive for national corporations. Eleutherian Mills, a du Pont home for five generations, has been restored as part of the museum. E. I. du Pont believed that the owner of a business should share the dangers facing his workers, and cracks in his home recall the tragic explosions that from time to time destroyed life and property during the mills' 120 years of operations.

Chief think tank of the Du Pont Company, the 147-acre Experimental Station lies across Brandywine Creek from the original black-powder mills and just beyond Walker's Mill, a textile producer from 1815 to the late 1930's.

Breakthroughs in treating cancer or the common cold could emerge from the Experimental Station as Du Pont focuses on molecular biology at its new Life Sciences Complex. Research physicist Edward Caruthers (right) joins the effort by study-ing how computers can be used to examine the structure and properties of DNA.

Earliest major port of call on the Delaware River, New Castle lost the bustle of commercial shipping by the early 19th century, but never surrendered its charm. Generations of homeowners have maintained residences gracing the Strand in the city's historic district. Other homes recall the influence of the Dutch, who began the settlement in 1651 as Fort Casimir. William Penn made his first New World stop here in 1682 to claim his grant of the three counties on the Delaware.

Delaware's political identity was forged in the New Castle County Court House, once the state's Colonial capitol. Restoration saved this 1732 landmark, which fell into disrepair after the county seat moved to Wilmington in 1881. The courthouse spire is the point from which surveyors drew Delaware's unique northern border—an arc with a 12-mile radius, then considered an average day's journey on horseback.

Tombstones dating from 1707 surround New Castle's Immanuel Episcopal Church, rededicated in December 1982 almost three years after fire destroyed all but its floor and outer walls. Contributions to rebuild the historic church came from across the state and country. "We couldn't have done it by ourselves," says parish rector Miles Edwards. The restored sanctuary interior now more closely resembles its appearance in 1820, when the transept and steeple were added.

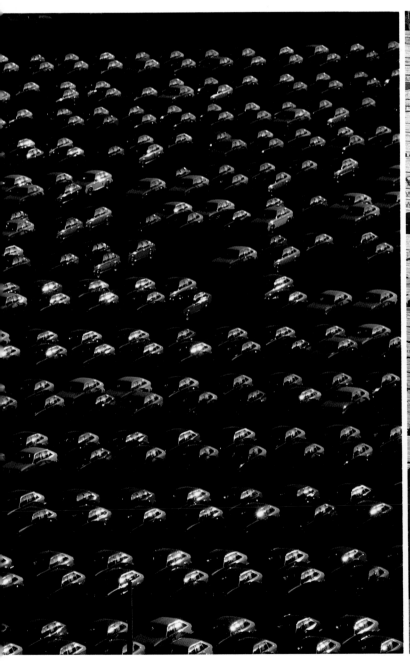

America's oldest company, J. E. Rhoads and Sons, supplies leather belting for the Hagley Museum Machine Shop, where its earliest known account book is here displayed (left). Originally founded in 1702, Rhoads moved to Delaware in 1867 and today produces the largest range of industrial belting in the U.S.

The Chrysler Corporation in Newark, Delaware and General Motors in nearby Newport (center) manufacture acres of new cars every year.

Lumber from British Columbia and fresh fruit from South America are distributed to the Northeast from the Port of Wilmington—now the nation's third largest banana port.

To paint perfect side stripes on a Gulfstream II, a crew at Atlantic Aviation must first put the rest of the jet under wraps. Based at the Greater Wilmington Airport in New Castle County, Atlantic Aviation is the oldest and one of the largest corporations devoted to business aviation sales and service, with branches now operating in six other states. Paint, furnishings, and avionics are custom tailored when clients purchase business aircraft such as this Israeli-built Westwind (left).

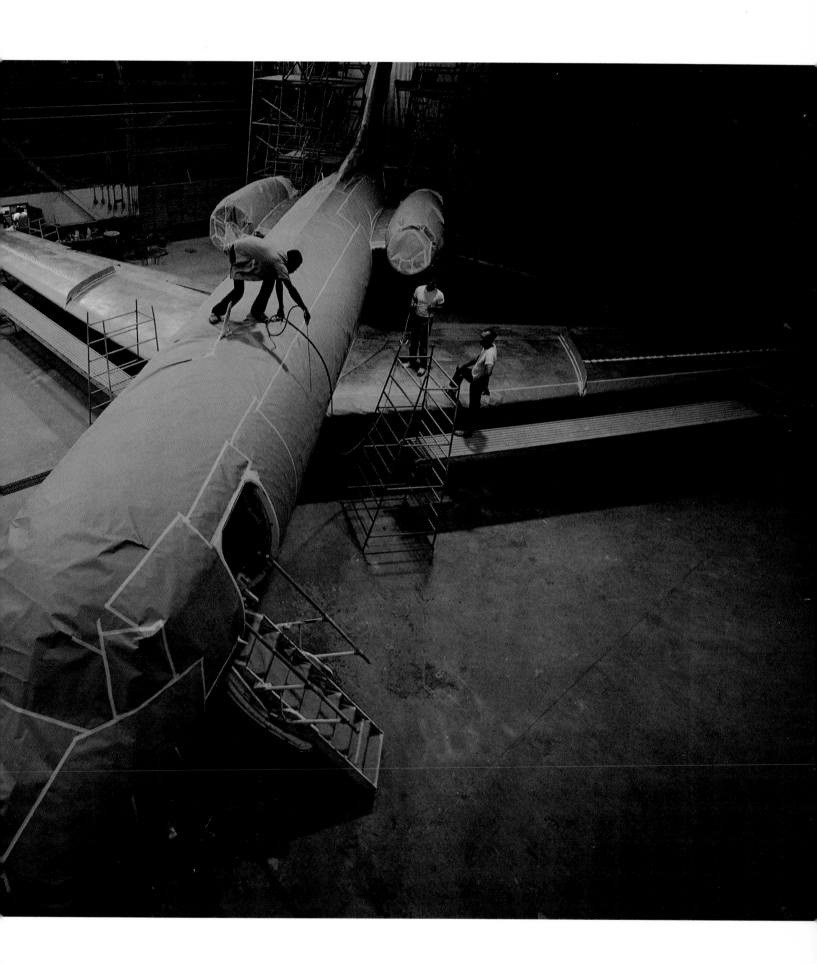

His ship loaded with a cargo of refined
fuel, a crewman casts off restraining lines
at the Getty Oil Refinery marine terminal
in Delaware City.

Industrial fireworks fly as Paul Young smoothes a steel dredge pipe fabricated at the Deemer Steel Casting Company in New Castle. Deemer has cast metal parts here since 1904, and its more than 30 members take pride in continuing Delaware's oldest local chapter of the United Steelworkers Union.

Commercial ventures of all sizes cross paths on the Delaware River, where a crab boat yields to a freighter traveling up one of the East Coast's busiest shipping lanes. In southern New Castle County, the river gives way to Delaware Bay, and the center of the ship channel becomes the state's boundary with neighboring New Jersey.

Launched in 1934 on the Christina River at Wilmington, the Coast Guard Cutter Mohawk patrolled the North Atlantic during World War II. Back on the river today, she is a museum and a memorial to that campaign and a symbol of the city's waterfront restoration.

Linked to the world by the Delaware River, the Getty Oil Refinery north of Delaware City can process 140,000 barrels of crude oil daily and is also a major producer of sulfur and methanol. Pipelines running from the refinery to its marine terminal carry crude oil from incoming tankers and return fuel products for domestic use and export.

Where northbound coastal Route 9 loses its scenic status, the Getty refinery marks the southern boundary of Delaware's heavy industries. In 1971, the state created the Coastal Zone Act—the first of its kind in the country—which prohibits new heavy industry from locating along the Delaware shoreline and the Chesapeake and Delaware Canal.

Mouth-watering dilemmas abound when Wilmington's Little Italy pulls out the stops for the annual St. Anthony's Festival. Volunteer balloon vendor Sister Ermanelda Hartdegen gets a hand from a famous Italian character during the week-long June event, which benefits the parish church, St. Anthony of Padua, in the heart of the close-knit community. Such festivals enliven the city throughout the year, as its many ethnic groups—including Poles, Greeks, Hispanics, Jews, Swedes, and Germans—celebrate their cultural heritage.

Having fun for a good cause, children swing past Rockford Park's water tower while adults shop for plants and crafts at the annual Flower Market. Sponsored by a Wilmington charity since 1921, the fair raises funds for Delaware children's agencies. Award-winning photographer Fred Comegys takes a spin to cover the May festivities for the *News-Journal*, the state's largest newspaper.

"I want things kept as they are because in fifty years nobody will know what a country place was," Henry Francis du Pont said of Winterthur, his birthplace and home, which he opened as a museum in 1951. The fifth-generation owner, du Pont in- herited the estate in 1926. It grew, as did his passion for antiques, into the world's largest collection of American decorative arts. The Winterthur collection includes entire rooms from other historic houses moved to Delaware to recreate interiors displaying more than 200 years of Ameri- can decorative arts and furnishings styles, beginning with the mid-17th century. A striking example is the Montmorenci Stair- case (left), built in a North Carolina home about 1822.

A folk-dance ensemble spins in a rollicking German courtship dance at the annual Winterthur Country Fair. The ten-kilometer race through the grounds kicks off the fall fair, proceeds from which aid in Winterthur's operation and further du Pont's desire that his home and the English gardens he meticulously cultivated should be "for the education and enjoyment of the public."

Microscopic analysis reveals clues for a painting's restoration in the training studio of the Winterthur Art Conservation Program—one of three leading programs of its kind in the country. Winterthur and the University of Delaware sponsor these courses and the country's most prestigious graduate study program which trains curators in American decorative arts.

Thoroughbreds stretch for victory at the Winterthur Point-to-Point Races run on the grounds of the 963-acre estate each May. Some 10,000 spectators turn out for this day in the country, which offers the devotee the finest in horse racing—and people watching.

Brandywine Creek forges through Delaware's piedmont, where autumn beauty here blurs the boundary with Pennsylvania. The region helped inspire the Brandywine School of Art, born a century ago in the Wilmington studio of famed illustrator Howard Pyle, and nourished since then by three generations of the Wyeth family. A major collection of works by these artists is in the Brandywine River Museum, just over the border in Chadds Ford.

The tradition of American realism fostered by the Brandywine School of Art continues with renowned Wilmington sculptor Charles Parks, whose works in bronze and steel grace buildings, churches, parks, and private collections across the United States and in Europe. His clay model of William Penn was cast as a seven-foot bronze for the city of New Castle to commemorate Penn's first New World landing.

In use since 1844, a moonlit horse barn embodies the country-quiet spirit of Delaware's rolling northern landscape.

Running in blue and gold, the University of Delaware's Fightin' Blue Hens have carried the ball to three national championships under head coach Tubby Raymond. The team's nickname salutes the state bird and Delaware's Revolutionary War troops, who won the sobriquet "Blue Hen's Chickens" for fighting with the zeal of that feisty gamecock.

Cornerstone of the University of Delaware, the white-columned Old College was founded in Newark in 1834 and today presides over a campus of 17,000 students. Long noted particularly for its research and teaching in engineering and agricultural sciences, the university has recently become known for pioneering work in solar energy and marine biology.

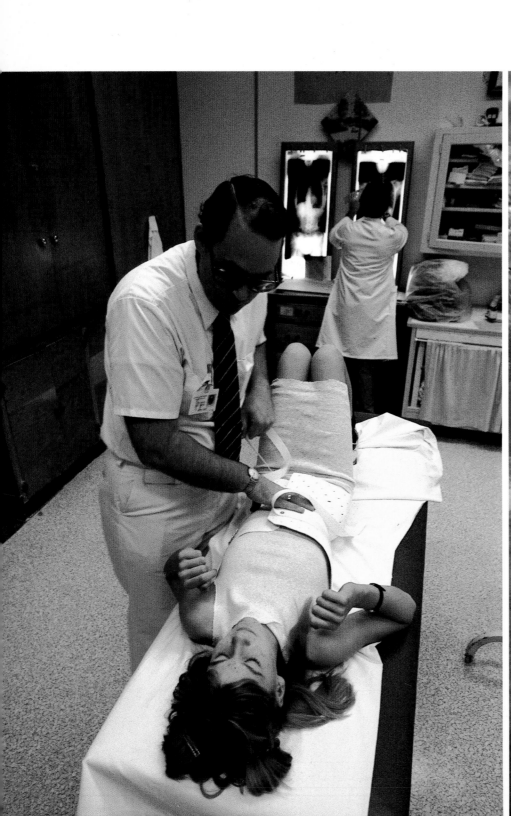

Advances in orthopedics and the treatment of childhood disorders have brought world attention to the Alfred I. du Pont Institute opened in 1940 on du Pont's 300-acre estate near Wilmington. Thousands of children now receive care at the Insti-

tute each year—many at no cost. Here, doctors researching disorders of the spinal column invented the scoliometer to measure curvature of the spine and replaced heavy corrective casts with a lightweight orthoplast jacket called the Wilmington

brace (left). The Institute's newly expanded facilities lie beyond the Carillon Tower (center), where Mr. du Pont was buried in 1935. His will created the Nemours Foundation as chief beneficiary of his extraordinary wealth. The foundation

also funds the Nemours Health Programs, serving senior citizens across Delaware.

A reflection of French elegance, his 77-room château was completed in 1910 and named Nemours after the du Pont ancestral home near Paris. From travels in Europe, du Pont carried home such art treasures as cast-iron gates made for Catherine the Great of Russia and a six-foot-tall musical clock thought to have belonged to Marie Antoinette. As a practical inventor who held more than 200 patents, du Pont designed his own electrical and heating systems and fitted his home with mechanical conveniences, including an ice maker and a spring-water bottling plant.

"I have never known a river, except the upper Thames, to be held by those who know it well in such affectionate regard." The Brandywine that inspired Delaware-born writer Henry Seidel Canby's idylls still flows for canoeists and floaters near Brandywine Creek State Park north of Wilmington.

Wheels of a sulky leave their signature on the Brandywine Raceway track as horse and jockey work out for evening pari-mutuel racing. Harness racing originated in Maryland and in New Jersey in the mid-18th century and undoubtedly caught on early in Delaware, where seasonal racing at three tracks makes it a nearly year-round sport. Thoroughbred, coaching, and steeplechase enthusiasts can be found throughout the state, and a new training facility will soon bring even more horses to Delaware Park in Stanton.

Practice paid off for the 1982 junior eight-member crew from St. Andrew's School in Middletown. As the 1983 varsity team, they placed second in their sport's most prestigious race, the Henley Royal Regatta in England. Built beside two-mile-long Noxontown Pond, the co-ed boarding school seems a natural site for champion rowing. Almost half of the 240 students benefit from scholarships endowed by members of the du Pont family, who founded St. Andrew's in 1927.

A child's imagination uncovers a super highway on the slick marsh grass of a New Castle embankment.

Where traffic is light, a marsh fisherman
enjoys his solitude south of Augustine
Beach on the last wooden bridge along
the state's scenic coastal road, Route 9.

The land has been good to Gordon Armstrong—farmer, hunter, and trapper —and he has returned the favor. For more than 30 years, he and his late wife watched over a colony of great blue herons on the Armstrongs' 240 acres near Augustine Beach, and farmed without pesticides that might contaminate the habitat of these birds, who nest from February to July. To insure protection of the 135-nest heronry, one of the region's largest, Armstrong sold his property in 1982 to Delaware Wild Lands, a private conservation group that now manages the land as the Armstrong Wildlife Preserve.

Crouched under natural cover, Fred Bonner scans the sky for geese at the dawn of the fall hunting season. Canada and snow geese, black ducks and Blue-wings, are among the migrants of the Atlantic Flyway that annually seek a temporary winter home in Delaware.

The Canal, to Delawareans, means the 13-mile-long Chesapeake and Delaware Canal, opened in 1829 to connect the Delaware River and Bay with the Chesapeake Bay. Bisecting New Castle County, the canal separates the state's urban north from its predominantly rural south. Four bridges in Delaware link "Upstate and Downstate," but often more than structural steel is needed to bridge the frequent political gaps existing between interest groups from above and below the canal.

Morning fog hugging only the ground north of St. Georges Bridge (left, below) might lend credence to the folklore that even the weather is different in the northern and southern parts of the state. That fog canopy all but hides the railroad bridge (top), rebuilt in 1966 when the Army Corps of Engineers widened the canal to 450 feet and dredged a 35-foot channel.

Wake within wake ripples the Chesapeake and Delaware Canal as boats bound for Maryland pass under Reedy Point Bridge. World-faring merchant ships as well as local pleasure craft take advantage of this nautical shortcut.

Fort Delaware never faced battle during its Army service from 1861 to 1944. Now a museum and state park, the granite pentagon centered in the Delaware River on Pea Patch Island saw heaviest duty as a Civil War prison for as many as 12,500 Confederate captives. Hundreds of thousands of egrets and herons today thrive in the marshland covering most of the island, one mile by boat off Delaware City.

Homebound in his authentic dress, a Union soldier draws 20th-century stares in Delaware City (left). Though Delaware officially sided with the Union as a border state, there were numerous southern sympathizers, and many families sent sons and cousins to fight for opposing sides. The state was among the last to free slaves after the war, yet its economy never depended heavily on slave labor. A Civil War sentry assumes his post on Pea Patch Island and mother and child don the style of another century when the Delaware Historical Re-enactment Society recreates Fort Delaware's prison era.

The textures of Odessa's historic district recall the halcyon days of this early Delaware port on Appoquinimink Creek. Two of Delaware's most beautiful homes, the Corbit-Sharp and Wilson-Warner Houses are now located here as part of Winter-thur Museum.

Serpentine stone distinguishes St. Anne's Episcopal Church (above), built in Middletown in 1882. Colonial Delaware apparently tested the faith of Anglican missionaries who founded this parish in 1705. One reported that his fellow priest, "Poor brother Jenkins . . . was baited to death by mosquitoes and blood thirsty Gal Knippers, which would not let him rest night nor day till he got a fever, came to Philadelphia, and died immediately."

Early winter casts its wistful spell over a farm south of St. Georges Bridge. The state's 49,000 acres of winter wheat take root during this usually moderate season.

Delaware statesman John M. Clayton finished his Greek Revival home in 1847 and named it Buena Vista after the site of General Zachary Taylor's victory that year in the Mexican War. Clayton later served as President Taylor's Secretary of State, and became Chief Justice and U.S. Senator for his native state. His heirs donated Buena Vista to Delaware in 1965 for use as a conference and reception center.

Sunset kindles a blaze in the windows of
a farmhouse near Odessa.

Rural silhouettes capture the dominant character of the state, more than 50 percent of which is farmland—the largest percentage for a state on the East Coast. Agriculture directly employs only three percent of the work force, but earnings make agriculture the third largest industry after manufacturing and tourism.

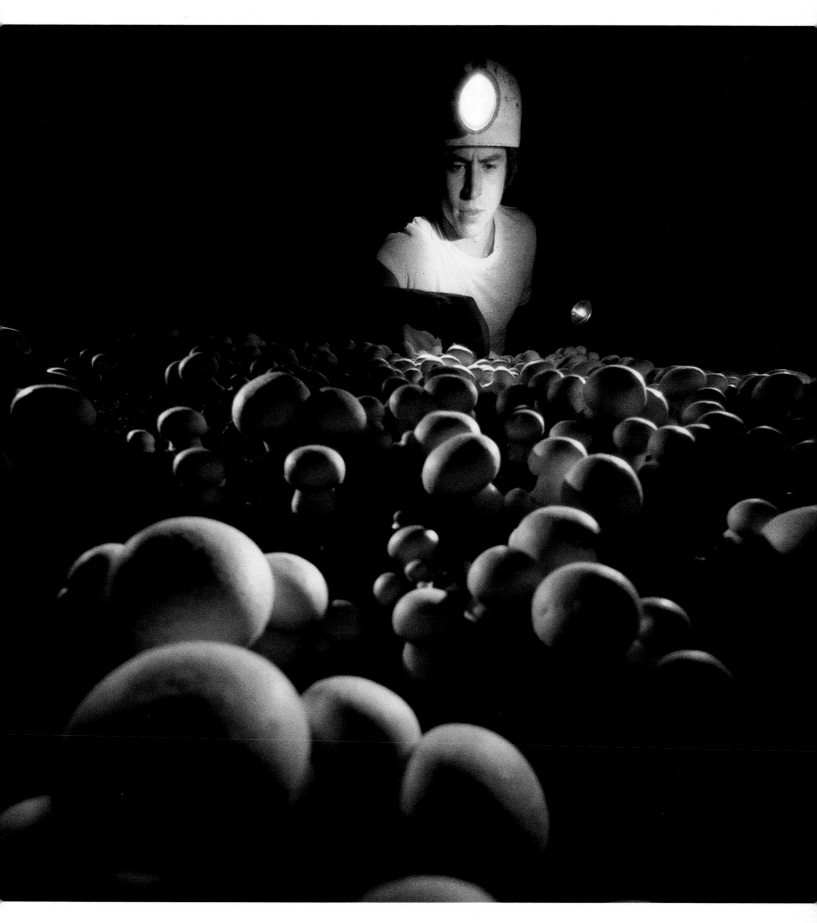

Kernels of corn rain over a farmworker in southern New Castle County as he lifts a board to spread the harvest in a truck bed. Soybeans and corn account for 90 percent of Delaware's tilled acreage and all but a fraction becomes feed for broiler chickens, the major source of farm income.

Third-generation mushroom grower Kevin Iaconi tends a 60-year-old family enterprise in Hockessin. The mushroom harvest of northern New Castle County ranks Delaware fourth in national production. Mushroom cultivation in the U.S. began late in the last century in Pennsylvania and soon crossed the border into Delaware.

Corn is still harvested minutes north of downtown Wilmington. Though agriculture claims an increasingly smaller niche here as farmland gives way to residential and business needs, large land holdings in state parks and private estates perpetuate the region's greenbelt.

John Doughty's green thumb brings a flowery welcome to three million people who stop each year at the Smyrna Rest Area on Route 13. Situated on this central artery on New Castle County's southern border, the Smyrna Rest Area offers recreation, food, tourist information, and an enclave of horticultural beauty to travelers bound upstate or down.

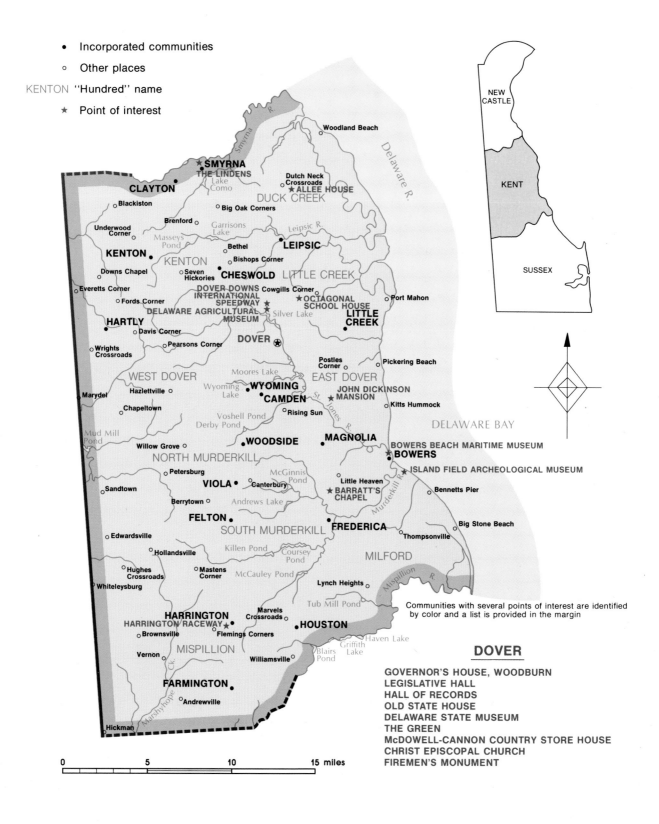

Incorporated communities

Other places

KENTON "Hundred" name

Point of interest

NEW CASTLE

KENT

SUSSEX

Woodland Beach

SMYRNA
THE LINDENS
CLAYTON
Lake Como
Dutch Neck Crossroads
ALLEE HOUSE
DUCK CREEK
Delaware R.

Blackiston
Big Oak Corners
Brenford
Garrisons Lake
Leipsic R.
Underwood Corner
Masseys Pond
KENTON
KENTON
Bethel
LEIPSIC
Bishops Corner
Downs Chapel
Seven Hickories
CHESWOLD
LITTLE CREEK
Everetts Corner
DOVER DOWNS INTERNATIONAL SPEEDWAY
Cowgills Corner
OCTAGONAL SCHOOL HOUSE
Port Mahon
Fords Corner
DELAWARE AGRICULTURAL MUSEUM
Silver Lake
LITTLE CREEK
HARTLY
Davis Corner
DOVER
Wrights Crossroads
Pearsons Corner
Postles Corner
Pickering Beach
WEST DOVER
Moores Lake
EAST DOVER
Marydel
Hazlettville
Wyoming Lake
WYOMING
JOHN DICKINSON MANSION
Chapeltown
CAMDEN
Kitts Hummock
Rising Sun
DELAWARE BAY
Voshell Pond
Derby Pond
MAGNOLIA
Mud Mill Pond
Willow Grove
WOODSIDE
BOWERS BEACH MARITIME MUSEUM
NORTH MURDERKILL
BOWERS
Petersburg
McGinnis Pond
ISLAND FIELD ARCHEOLOGICAL MUSEUM
Sandtown
VIOLA
Canterbury
Little Heaven
Bennetts Pier
Berrytown
Andrews Lake
BARRATT'S CHAPEL
FELTON
SOUTH MURDERKILL
FREDERICA
Big Stone Beach
Edwardsville
Killen Pond
Coursey Pond
MILFORD
Thompsonville
Hollandsville
Hughes Crossroads
Mastens Corner
McCauley Pond
Lynch Heights
Whiteleysburg
Tub Mill Pond

Communities with several points of interest are identified by color and a list is provided in the margin

HARRINGTON
Marvels Crossroads
HOUSTON
HARRINGTON RACEWAY
Haven Lake
Brownsville
Flemings Corners
Griffith Lake
Vernon
MISPILLION
Blairs Pond
Williamsville

FARMINGTON
Andrewville

Hickman

DOVER

GOVERNOR'S HOUSE, WOODBURN
LEGISLATIVE HALL
HALL OF RECORDS
OLD STATE HOUSE
DELAWARE STATE MUSEUM
THE GREEN
McDOWELL-CANNON COUNTRY STORE HOUSE
CHRIST EPISCOPAL CHURCH
FIREMEN'S MONUMENT

0   5   10   15 miles

KENT

The verdant heart of Delaware, Kent is the state's central county and home to the capital city of Dover. Superlatives describe this region's diversity.

Half the U.S. fleet of C-5A Galaxies—the world's largest airplane—is stationed near the capitol at Dover Air Force Base.

Here, along Delaware Bay, lies the state's greatest concentration of wildlife preserves, dominated by Bombay Hook, Delaware's first and largest national wildlife refuge.

Most of Delaware's potatoes, its major truck crop, are grown in Kent County, and most of the Delaware watermen who ply the bay and river for blue crabs, fish, and oysters work out of Kent County's small-town ports.

When Space Shuttle astronauts made their historic untethered space walk, they were wearing suits whose components were manufactured at ILC Dover. Such light manufacturing has grown to play a key role in the county's economy since World War II, and Dover, its largest city, has emerged as a major retail center for the Delmarva Peninsula.

But half of Kent remains farmland, and the county still turns to the bounty of its earth and waters. Kent hosts the State Fair each summer and, appropriately, is home to the Delaware Agricultural Museum, opened in 1980 north of Dover to preserve the state's farming heritage and its traditional craftsmanship.

Visions of farming past linger west of Dover, where more than 225 Old Order Amish families follow the ways of their forebears who settled in Kent County early in this century.

Dawn flight prep at Dover Air Force Base readies the world's largest airplanes, C-5A Galaxies, designed to carry outsize military equipment. The busiest military cargo port on the East Coast, Dover AFB operates half of the U.S. C-5A fleet and the nation's largest military mortuary.

If ghosts are the measure of a home's character, Woodburn's is rich indeed. Built by a wealthy Dover landowner about 1790, this fine example of Georgian architecture (left) possessed a legendary host of specters when the state restored it as the Governor's House in 1966. Republican Governor Pierre S. "Pete" du Pont (1977–85) startled Halloween trick-or-treaters here as Dracula, and invited the state to an annual Governor's Fair on Woodburn's grounds, where here he faces the hazards of an egg-toss contest.

Under the graceful cupola of the new Legislative Hall, senators and representatives of the General Assembly have met since 1934.

Second oldest state capitol in continuous use, the State House was built on Dover's historic Green between 1787 and 1792. Until the General Assembly outgrew these quarters, legislators ascended to their chambers on the staircases flanking tour guide Hattie Mae Biddle, pictured here. A portion of the state's archives is now preserved in the State House.

The General Assembly first met in Dover in 1777 when New Castle seemed vulnerable to river attack by the British. After much regional bickering, Dover became the permanent capital in 1781. Here, the General Assembly made Delaware the First State on December 7, 1787, since it was first to ratify the U.S. Constitution.

Microfiche records of 150,000 Delaware corporations—including more than half the Fortune 500—are overseen in Dover by Corporate Administrator Marie Shultie. Though few of these companies keep in-state headquarters, they incorporate here to benefit from a model set of incorporation laws. Their annual fees and franchise taxes now supply ten percent of the state's annual revenue. The legal expertise of Delaware's Court of Chancery, devoted to equity issues, gives corporate plaintiffs and defendants quick access to judicial hearings. Only three other states—Arkansas, Mississippi, and Tennessee—retain a separate chancery court, a derivative of the centuries-old English system of justice.

The governing body of Kent County retains the traditional name of Levy Court, reflecting the commissioners' power to levy taxes. Kent County last increased its property-tax rate in 1974, and property taxes across Delaware rank among the lowest in the nation. Before the start of the weekly Levy Court meeting in Dover, county attorney Max Terry catches up on the news of his trade.

Delaware Chief Justice Daniel L. Herrmann (right) heads the five-justice Supreme Court, which reviews appeals from the Court of Chancery and other lower courts. Even on the bench he follows the bow tie precedent set by the late U.S. Supreme Court justice Thomas C. Clark.

Seasonal blossoms accent the charms of Dover (left, above), Delaware's third largest city after Wilmington and Newark. In 1683, William Penn ordered that Dover be created as the county seat of Kent, and streets were laid out in 1717. Each May,

Old Dover Days celebrate the city's rich past with a weekend of Colonial-era activities and tours of historic homes. Three centuries of Delaware history are displayed year-round in the state's museums.

"You can get almost anything almost

anytime," seems to be the motto of Spence's Bazaar in Dover (left and above), a lively cross of farmers' market, auction, and yard sale run by the Spence family since 1933.

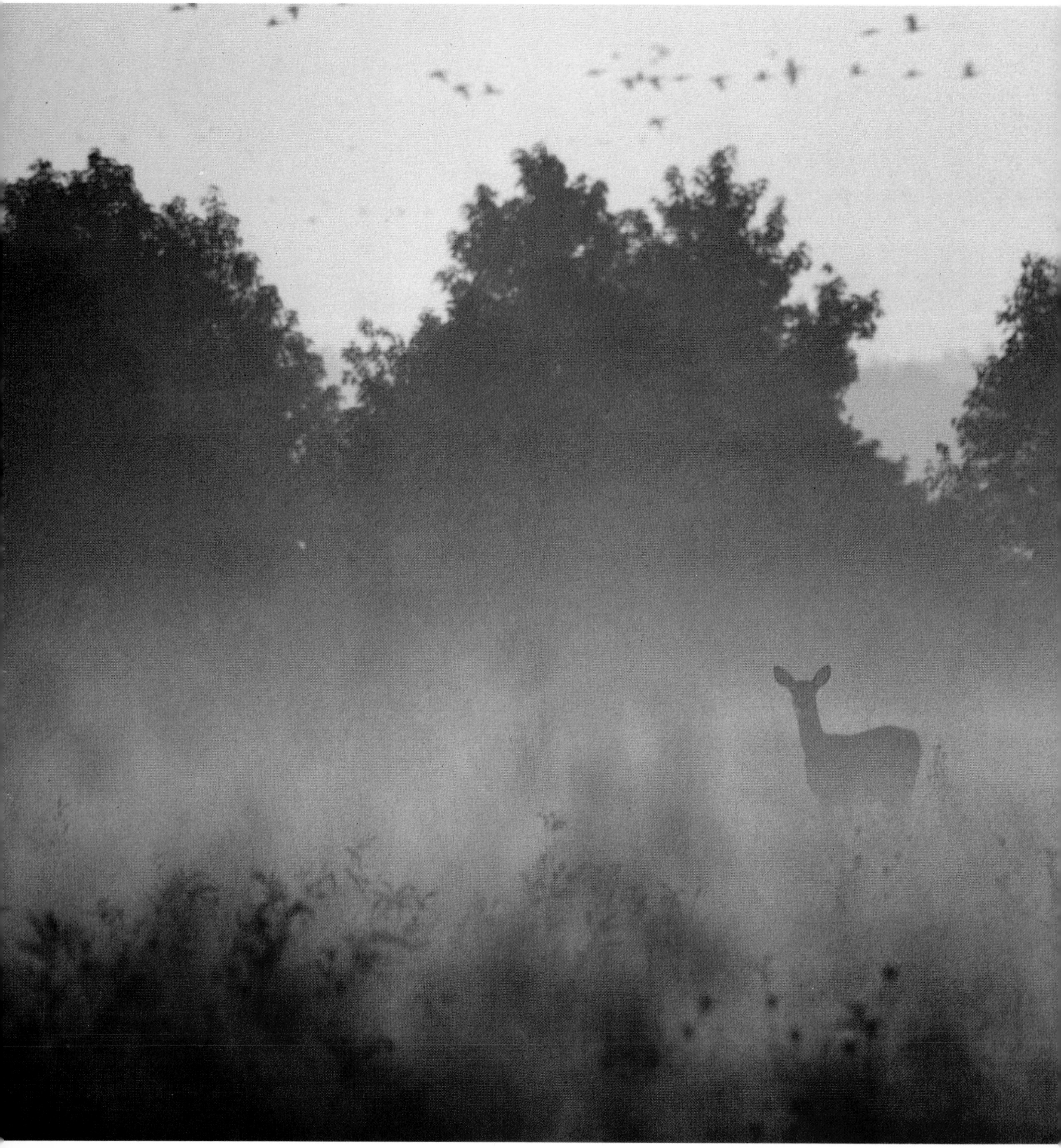

A deer blends with the doeskin hues that autumn paints on Bombay Hook National Wildlife Refuge, 15,000 acres on Delaware Bay preserved since 1937 for such year-round inhabitants and for migrating birds along the Atlantic Flyway. As many as 200,000 Canada and snow geese descend each fall on Bombay Hook and Prime Hook National Wildlife Refuges, and on the many state-managed preserves.

Great egrets stalk fish, snakes, frogs, and
crayfish in Bombay Hook National Wildlife Refuge.

Prized sighting for Bombay Hook bird-watchers, a black-crowned night heron rests at dawn after nocturnal feeding.

Space suits for the Apollo and Skylab programs were launched at ILC Dover, where test subject Tom Knapp works out in a suit designed for Space Shuttle astronauts. ILC Dover builds most of the parts for the modular Space Shuttle suit, later assembled by NASA. Material for these suits, worn during space walks, was developed by another Delaware company, W. L. Gore and Associates, well known for its foul-weather material called Gore-Tex.

Every day, tons of coconut meat from the Philippines and chocolate chips by the millions are processed, blended, and packaged at the General Foods Corporation plant in Dover, one of Kent County's largest employers. The company has recently begun work on an innovative co-generation project, which will provide electricity and steam to the plant and surplus electricity for the neighboring Dover community.

April to November, watermen break before dawn to trap delectable blue crabs in the Delaware River and Bay. Most crabbers also set traps for eels—sold for crab bait or shipped to European food markets —and set gill nets for perch, rockfish, shad, and trout in the late winter and spring.

With prices and productivity ever fickle, life on the water is a gamble. Few chance it; fewer still can afford to follow the traditional waterman's cycle, which, in winter, turns to muskrat trapping on the marshes.

Oystering was the lifeblood of coastal towns until a parasite devastated the bay beds in the 1950s. Restocked, the estuary again yields these salty delicacies, now only a fraction of the former harvest. Banking on grit, luck, and optimism—and driven by a love of independence—Delaware watermen survive. "This is all I've ever done since I was a teeny boy," explains one. "I guess you don't have to make too much money if you're doing what you want to do."

The pursuit of blue crabs sends pipe-smoking Harry Killen and his crewman Mike Slaughter from Leipsic on daily rounds through the Delaware Bay and River. "I love what I do, that's for sure," says Killen, a veteran of 36 years on the water. "I guess that's why I'm still at it."

On another boat out of Leipsic, crewman Jimper Fox (center) unloads and rebaits a crab pot. A good day's catch might bring 15 to 20 bushels, but demand is always higher. "I wish I could serve only Delaware crabs—I really think we have the best—but I have to buy a lot from the Chesapeake," says Sam Burrows (right), who opened his popular Leipsic restaurant in 1953 and gave it his childhood nickname—Sambo's.

Potato digging leaves its dusty badge on a farmhand, drawing the last puff from his afternoon break. Harvesters ride through the field with a mechanical digger, picking out stones and dirt clods before the potatoes roll into the side truck. Kent County grows most of the state's potatoes, Delaware's major truck crop.

Second reapers of the corn harvest, geese flock from wildlife refuges to feed on nearby farms. Mechanical harvesters leave ample amounts of corn behind, and Delaware's goose population in winter has soared with the increase in corn and soybean farming during the past 40 years.

A lifetime of working the water is reflected on the face of the late Sammy Martin —oysterman, fisherman, and dockhand for charter boats in the bay-side town of Bowers Beach.

Charter boats line the Murderkill River dock in Bowers Beach, the northernmost port of Delaware's multimillion-dollar sportfishing industry. Fronting Delaware Bay between the mouths of the Murderkill and St. Jones rivers, Bowers Beach was named by landowner John Bowers in the 1740's, and became a popular summer resort in the late 19th century, when steamships brought visitors from as far away as Philadelphia. Summer-cottage residents today double the population of this town of 200 people.

Charter boats head out of Bowers Beach from May to October, setting their lines for weakfish (sea trout), flounder, bluefish, and sea bass. At the height of sea trout season in late May or early June, the city of Milford sponsors the World Championship Weakfish Tournament.

Sharks, once thrown back or brought in only as souvenirs, have earned more respect from charter boat crews and fishermen as shark fillets grow in popularity. Six shark species swim off Delaware's Atlantic Coast, and the dogfish and sandbar shark come into Delaware Bay. Cleaned and iced immediately, all but the hammerhead and sand shark are considered great eating.

Reaping fresh air—and fish—Amish from Pennsylvania make a day of charter boating on Delaware Bay.

A virtual ghost town during the winter, South Bowers Beach (above) remains an out-of-the-way haven of summer cottages on the bay. To preserve their isolation, summer residents decades ago fought off proposals to build a bridge linking them to Bowers Beach on the opposite bank of the Murderkill River.

Grandest of Kent County's plantation manors, the boyhood home of Revolutionary War statesman John Dickinson was built about 1740 on the fertile land of Jones Neck south of Dover. Dickinson's father was among the English planters who moved during this era from Maryland into Kent and Sussex counties and began large-scale cultivation of grain and, for a few years, tobacco.

But law, not farming, attracted John Dickinson, who wrote influential tracts questioning British taxation and became known as "the penman of the Revolution." The pre-constitutional political structure allowed him to serve as Delaware's chief executive and then as governor of Pennsylvania. This side view of his home—one of many historic Kent County sites restored and open to the public—contrasts the glazed Flemish bond brickwork of the main house with less costly patterns used for later additions.

Considered the "cradle of Methodism" in America, Barratt's Chapel (above), near Frederica, has held services since 1780. Here, evangelist Francis Asbury met in 1784 with a representative of John Wesley and helped foster the founding of the Methodist Episcopal Church later that year in Baltimore. Richard Allen, a freed Kent County slave, later organized one of the largest black American denominations, the African Methodist Episcopal Church, in Philadelphia.

Burial ground of Revolutionary War patriot Caesar Rodney, Dover's Christ Episcopal Church (right) was founded in 1704 by Rodney's grandfather, a Church of England missionary. The brick sanctuary used today dates from the mid-1730's.

Marian Hitchens of Laurel and her lamb, Sunshine (left), lost to the cows in the Pretty Animal Contest at the Delaware State Fair, but, as a market lamb, her 4-H project took second place. More than 10,000 exhibitors display the best efforts of farm homes and fields during the nine-day State Fair, held every July on the 253-acre fairgrounds in Harrington. But you don't have to win to have a great time in the greased-pole climbing contest (center) or among the acres of games and rides on the Midway (right).

Most state fairs are state financed, but Delaware's has operated as a nonprofit organization since it was first incorporated as the Kent and Sussex Fair in 1919. Attendance now tops 200,000 people.

Colorful standout in a crowd of Holsteins, a Guernsey cow tolerates a head-to-tail grooming from Sue Ann McClements for State Fair competition. A day at the fair begins as early as a workday on the farm.

Tommy Eliason gets a headstart by bunking with his Jersey cows (center). Only about 40 Guernseys and 80 Jerseys are kept in Delaware, and their rich milk usually goes for a family's personal use. The low-fat milk given by Delaware's 12,000 Holsteins supplies the small but productive dairy industry, recently honored when milk was named the official state beverage.

Among 175 hog contenders at the fair, three red Durocs snuggled in their pen. Sussex County raises most of the state's 33,000 hogs.

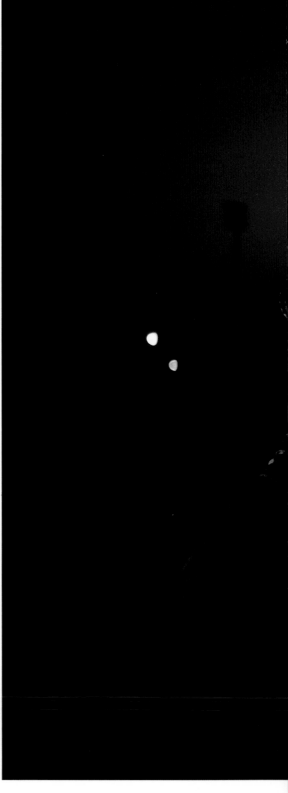

Vision takes second place to style as children imitate the fashion of rodeo cowboys
at the State Fair.

Professional cowboys of the American Rodeo Association relax in the State Fair Grandstand before their hard-driving show. Daily Grandstand shows include rodeo acts and stock-car races, tractor pulls, and demolition derbies, and feature many popular entertainers such as Conway Twitty, Kool and the Gang, and Dolly Parton.

Grand National stock-car racing heats up Dover Downs International Speedway when drivers such as the Pettys, Allisons, and Yarboroughs tackle the Budweiser 500 in May and the Delaware 500 in September—races on the championship circuit that begins every year with the Daytona 500. Crowds of more than 40,000 people spill into the infield, where spectators huddle to follow radio broadcasts while a lone fan takes the pole position atop his camper.

Witness to the heyday and decline of Delaware Bay oystering, the now-abandoned Port Mahon Lighthouse was built in the early 19th century at the southern end of Delaware's 15-mile-long natural oyster beds. Seed is still harvested from here to stock new beds.

Dawn beckons a waterman's bow down the Leipsic River toward Delaware Bay.

Every twisting inch a keeper for dinner,
an eel delights its catcher fishing the
marsh near Woodland Beach.

Grant Armistead slices through Dover's Silver Lake, created on the St. Jones River during the last century to power a sawmill that supplied lumber to Civil War shipbuilders in the mid-Atlantic. Virtu-ally all of the Delaware lakes and ponds that now entice canoeists, power boaters, and skiers were formed by some of the state's early industries—grist and lumber mills.

The last light of day kisses the Miah Maull Shoal Lighthouse anchored just outside the shipping channel in Delaware Bay. Built in Wilmington in 1913, the 59-foot-tall cast-iron lighthouse was then moved to its present location to mark this shoal named for Nehemiah Maull, a Delaware River pilot whose ship is said to have sunk here in the late 18th century.

The sun winks at summer romance along
the St. Jones River, spiked with the ruins
of a Bowers Beach pier and an oyster-
shucking house.

Every boy in shouting distance makes the starting lineup for a sandlot baseball game in Leipsic, a town of little more than 200 people fronting the river that bears its name. The Muddy and Herring branches are home to hundreds of hunters in the fall and to fishermen nearly year round.

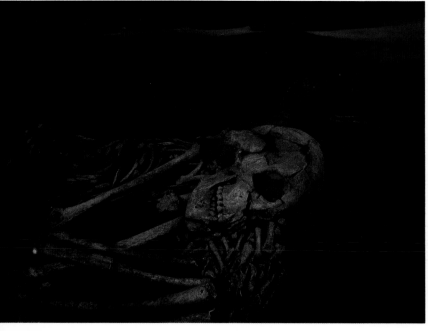

The prehistoric cemetery of Delaware's earliest known settlement came to light in 1967 along the Murderkill River and Delaware Bay. The history of these early Americans remains elusive, but between A.D. 500 and 1000 they hunted, fished, and farmed on this site now known as Island Field. Their artifacts, and those left across the state by nomadic hunters thousands of years earlier, fill the Island Field Museum, where 125 burials are displayed *in situ* under a transparent cover.

A concrete base supports the oak-slatted dome of the Cherbourg Round Barn (right), built by a dairy farmer in 1914 near Little Creek. Listed on the National Register of Historic Places, the architectural rarity is still used for storage on the farm.

A practiced eye helps Cathy Halderman call the shots at the Heart Break Hotel, where floods have played havoc with the floor level. "Folks would be all over me if I fixed it," says Sis Bolen, owner of this popular Bowers Beach restaurant and inn.

A gravel pit became playing fields for the Smyrna and Clayton Little League teams thanks to the efforts of state senator and veteran Little League coach James T. Vaughn (center), honored and surprised when the park was given his name.

Some people in Magnolia complained about "that pumpkin house," but Mayor Shirley Huddleston Jarrell—here with her son D. R.—stuck by her brushes when she painted her home, built by a wealthy peach grower at the turn of the century.

A day's farming done, Lister Hall, Jr., surveys a golden world from his home near Bowers Beach.

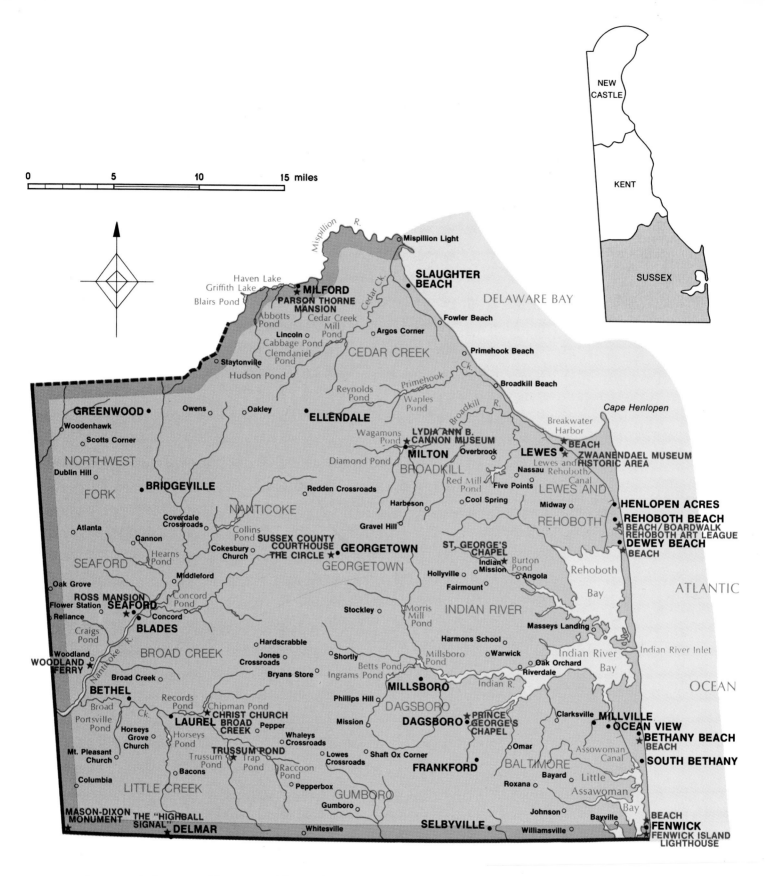

NEW CASTLE

KENT

SUSSEX

0   5   10   15 miles

Mispillion R.

Mispillion Light

SLAUGHTER BEACH

DELAWARE BAY

Haven Lake
Griffith Lake
Blairs Pond
MILFORD
PARSON THORNE MANSION
Abbotts Pond
Cedar Creek Mill Pond
Lincoln
Cabbage Pond
Clemdaniel Pond
Staytonville
Hudson Pond

Cedar Ck.

CEDAR CREEK

Fowler Beach

Argos Corner

Primehook Beach

Broadkill Beach

Cape Henlopen

GREENWOOD
Woodenhawk
Scotts Corner

Owens
Oakley

ELLENDALE

Reynolds Pond
Waples Pond

Primehook

Ck.

Broadkill R.

Breakwater Harbor

NORTHWEST

FORK

Dublin Hill

BRIDGEVILLE

Atlanta
Cannon

Coverdale Crossroads

Collins Pond

Cokesbury Church

Wagamons Pond
LYDIA ANN B. CANNON MUSEUM
MILTON
Diamond Pond
BROADKILL

Redden Crossroads

Harbeson

Gravel Hill

Overbrook
Red Mill Pond
Five Points
Nassau
Cool Spring

LEWES
BEACH
ZWAANENDAEL MUSEUM
HISTORIC AREA
Lewes and Rehoboth Canal

LEWES AND

REHOBOTH

Midway

HENLOPEN ACRES
REHOBOTH BEACH
BEACH/BOARDWALK
REHOBOTH ART LEAGUE
DEWEY BEACH
BEACH

NANTICOKE

Hearns Pond

SEAFORD

SUSSEX COUNTY COURTHOUSE
THE CIRCLE
GEORGETOWN

GEORGETOWN

ST. GEORGE'S CHAPEL
Indian Mission
Hollyville
Fairmount

Burton Pond
Angola

Rehoboth Bay

ATLANTIC

Oak Grove
Flower Station
Reliance
ROSS MANSION
SEAFORD
Middleford
Concord Pond
Concord
BLADES

Stockley

Morris Mill Pond

INDIAN RIVER

Masseys Landing

Indian River Inlet

Craigs Pond
Woodland
WOODLAND FERRY
BETHEL

Broad Creek

Hardscrabble
Jones Crossroads
Bryans Store

Shortly

Betts Pond
Ingrams Pond

Millsboro Pond

Harmons School

Warwick

Oak Orchard
Riverdale

Indian River Bay

OCEAN

BROAD CREEK

Records Pond
Chipman Pond
CHRIST CHURCH
BROAD CREEK
LAUREL
Pepper

Broad Ck.
Portsville Pond
Horseys Grove Church
Horseys Pond
TRUSSUM POND
Trussum Pond
Trap Pond

Whaleys Crossroads
Lowes Crossroads
Shaft Ox Corner

Phillips Hill

Mission

MILLSBORO

DAGSBORO

DAGSBORO
PRINCE GEORGE'S CHAPEL

Omar

Indian R.

Clarksville
MILLVILLE
OCEAN VIEW
BETHANY BEACH
BEACH
SOUTH BETHANY

Mt. Pleasant Church
Columbia
Bacons
Raccoon Pond
Pepperbox

FRANKFORD

BALTIMORE

Bayard
Roxana

Assowoman Canal

Little Assawoman Bay

LITTLE CREEK

GUMBORO

Gumboro

Johnson

Bayville

BEACH

MASON-DIXON MONUMENT
THE "HIGHBALL SIGNAL"
DELMAR

Whitesville

SELBYVILLE

Williamsville

FENWICK
FENWICK ISLAND LIGHTHOUSE

• Incorporated communities

CEDAR CREEK "Hundred" name

○ Other places

★ Point of interest

SUSSEX

Almost half of Delaware's land area lies in Sussex County, where the state reaches its maximum 35-mile width. Leading the state in farm production and summer tourism, Sussex stretches from a surf-struck Atlantic shore and placid bay coast across ribbon-flat fields planted most heavily in soybeans, corn, and melons. Here, in the birthplace of the modern poultry industry, thousands of streamlined chicken houses raise more broiler chickens than in any other U.S. county.

The number of visitors to Delaware's small-town Atlantic beach resorts soared after 1952 when the Chesapeake Bay Bridge brought quick access to the Delmarva Peninsula. The county's year-round population, now 98,000, has become the fastest-growing in the state. Retirees, settling largely in the beach communities, account for much of the 22 percent population increase since 1970. The largest city remains Seaford, where Du Pont operates the world's largest nylon plant.

Crossroads communities with names such as Hardscrabble and Shaft Ox Corner recall the historically rugged isolation of Sussex County, where oxen were common beasts of burden at the turn of the century. Agribusiness, tourism, and modern travel and communications have changed that life, but the tenacious, conservative, and gracious down-home spirit of Sussex County endures.

The high tide of summer tourism brings more than 100,000 weekend visitors to Delaware's Sussex County beaches. Here, in Rehoboth Beach, the largest Atlantic shore town, the year-round population of 1,730 makes a seasonal leap to 50,000 people. So many of these sunseekers hail from Washington, D.C., that Rehoboth Beach has become known as the "Nation's Summer Capital."

Simple pleasures of impromptu dancing and a cold beer form the stuff of summer memories in Dewey Beach, named for Spanish-American War hero Admiral George Dewey. The first summer hotel on the shore was built here in 1870, but development took hold on the higher ground in adjacent Rehoboth Beach, where, in 1873, delegates to a Methodist Church camp meeting laid out the town among groves of holly and loblolly pine. Though the "resort with religious influences" envisioned by these founders soon veered toward the secular, Rehoboth polishes an image as a family resort. Alcohol is forbidden on the beach and the boardwalk (above)—a mile-and-a-quarter-long—promenade of summer dreams.

First prize for sparking a child's imagination seems to go to this palatial entry in
the annual Rehoboth Beach Sandcastle
Building Contest, held the first Saturday
in August.

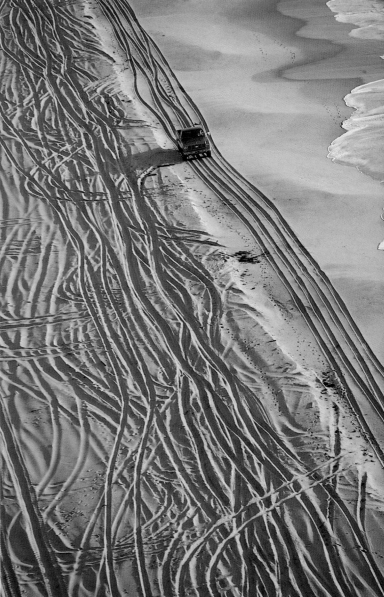

Tracks furrowed by surf-fishing vehicles vanish when high tide washes over the seven-mile-long Delaware Seashore State Park.

Most peaceful of Delaware's ocean resort towns, Bethany Beach (above) retains a quiet profile befitting its origins as a summer church retreat. Seeking a "safe and rational way of spending the heated term," Christian Church members selected this site in 1900 and sponsored a nationwide contest to choose its name. An oceanfront lot went to the winner from Chicago.

The summer population now exceeds 12,000 in contrast to the 330 winter residents. Sea Colony, a hotly debated condominium built in the 1970's, now towers over neighboring South Bethany (right). "I still can't get used to seeing it," says one woman, "but we're lucky they did a nice job."

Lured by Delaware's new banking laws, First Maryland Bancorp transformed a vacant factory in Millsboro into offices for two subsidiaries—First Omni Bank and First Delaware Services Corporation, whose computers here process checks and other customer-account data.

The recipe hasn't changed since 1926 when Ralph and Paul Adams set up shop in Bridgeville to make Rapa Brand scrapple —traditional Delaware breakfast meat of pork livers, hearts, trimmings, fatback, and seasoned flour.

No U.S. county grows more chickens than Sussex. The modern broiler-chicken industry was born here in 1923 when Cecile Steel of Ocean View first raised chickens year-round. "Broilers"—over 180,000,000 of them in 1982—now account for more than half of Delaware's agricultural income. Aspiring managers for this industry can study in the Poultry Technology Program at Delaware Technical and Community College near Georgetown, where Willis Kirk, one of Delaware's 1,200 chicken growers, here teaches an attentive class (left). Virtually all of the state's growers work under contract to one of nine Delmarva poultry companies, the largest of which is headed by Frank Perdue (right).

Tapping the healing power of Delaware Bay, the Barcroft Company in Lewes pumps in saltwater and extracts an antacid —magnesium hydroxide. Flanked by sand-filtering tanks, G. B. Glasscock, Vice-President of Chemical Operations and Engineering, checks a solution used to monitor the extraction process.

Barcroft yearly ships millions of pounds of magnesium hydroxide and aluminum hydroxide to pharmaceutical companies around the world. A large amount of these soothing compounds are made into Maalox by Barcroft's parent company, William H. Rorer of Pennsylvania.

The world's first and largest commercial nylon plant was opened in Seaford in 1939 by the Du Pont Company, which holds the patent on this first totally man-made fiber invented by their scientist Wallace H. Carothers. One of nearly 3,000 plant employees, merge operator Arnold Davis here scans for inconsistencies in a dye lot. Running every day, around the clock, the Seaford plant blends and spins nylon yarn for almost every use except perhaps its most famous one—stockings.

Nutter Marvel, a longtime Sussex resident and guardian of transportation's past, owns a famous collection of nearly 100 horse-drawn vehicles. Each Return Day, the Governor rides in one of Marvel's finest coaches, leading a parade of candidates, floats, and marching bands.

Old-fashioned politics reign on Return Day in Georgetown, the Thursday after Election Day, when town crier Ronnie Dodd reads the tallies from the balcony of the Sussex County Courthouse. A carry-over from an era when people had to travel to the county seat to hear election news, Return Day draws winners and losers from across the state to celebrate and become reconciled.

Modeled on the town hall of Hoorn in the Netherlands, the Zwaanendael Museum was built in Lewes in 1931 to commemorate the 300th anniversary of the first European settlement in Delaware. This site at the mouth of Delaware Bay was known as Zwaanendael—valley of the swans—to the Dutch who established a 28-man patroonship here in 1631. A reprisal by local Indians soon wiped out their venture, but in 1659 Dutch settlers succeeded in putting down the roots of modern-day Lewes, a harbor town of 2,200 people.

A moment of private reflection prepares a woman for an evening Methodist revival service at Carey's Camp near Millsboro. For ten days of midsummer fellowship, families open up 47 tiny houses, called tents, which face an open-frame taber- nacle. Hundreds of other worshipers ar- rive daily for services and Bible classes. Today's campground dates from 1888, but the site was used for meetings perhaps as early as the 1830's. Only four camp meet- ing grounds uphold this once widespread tradition in Delaware. "People have strong attachments to Carey's Camp," says one man. "Maybe that's why it endures. It's like the hymn we sing, 'Precious memories, how they linger, and how they ever flood my soul.'"

Loblolly pines and cypress trees in Trap Pond State Park set the scene for a joyous baptism service held by the Holiness Pentecostal Church of Lincoln, Delaware.

Farmers and their offspring follow fast-paced bidding at the Laurel Farmers' Auction Market, where more than two million dollars worth of melons change hands each summer. Truckloads of watermelons purchased by 20 major brokers and hundreds of smaller wholesalers wait to be loaded into tractor trailers that carry the crop—Delaware's largest fruit harvest—to Northeast markets (right).

Farmers formed the Southern Delaware Truck Growers Association in 1940. Stockholders today number nearly 1,600. Produce such as peppers, cucumbers, tomatoes, and pumpkins is also auctioned, but watermelons, cantaloupes, and honeydew melons predominate.

Harvests of Super Star cantaloupes and Sugar Baby watermelons wait in the selling line at the Laurel Farmers' Auction Market. The line stretches as much as a mile from the bidding platform on busiest days when 600 to 700 growers, and as many buyers, descend on the twelve-and-a-half-acre auction grounds. About half of these growers come from surrounding Maryland counties. Most of Delaware's melons grow in Sussex County.

Mountains of green beans fresh from Delaware fields await processing at the Draper Canning Company in Milton. The nation's largest independent cannery, Draper contracts for 33,000 acres of Delaware farmland and buys on the open market to can vegetables under 2,200 brand labels, including its own, King-Cole.

At the last water-powered grist mill in Delaware (right), owner Jacob Hearn Moore pitches in to spread unground corn in a storage bin atop the Hearn and Rawlins Flour Mill, run by his family in Seaford since 1885. Local markets sell the mill's white flour, cornmeal, and pancake mixes, but scrapple plants are its chief customers, buying 10,000 pounds of white flour and 20,000 pounds of cornmeal each week.

Hiking out, crew members reach for speed and victory in the Governor's Cup Race (above), a Lightning regatta held each June in Rehoboth Bay. Though little more than seven feet deep, Rehoboth Bay is one of the deepest inland bays on the East Coast, and, from early spring through fall, its waters bloom with small-craft sails, water skiers, fishermen, and crabbers.

Even in carefree moments sailors out of Lewes
mind conditions at the mouth of Delaware Bay,
where the tide changes with a fury and heavy
shoaling has frustrated navigators since the time
of Henry Hudson, who quickly abandoned his
mission to explore these waters in 1609.

Sunset over Lewes harbor silhouettes the tower of the Lightship Overfalls (right), one of the last of the floating light stations that once marked East Coast hazards and now houses a museum of maritime history. Lewes early on became known for pilots who maneuvered merchant vessels up the estuary. Today, Lewes remains a headquarters for Delaware River pilots who, by law, must guide ships and tankers bound for Wilmington, Philadelphia, and Camden.

"We're trying to find out how the Delaware estuary works," explains Dr. Jonathan Sharp (foreground), associate professor at the University of Delaware College of Marine Studies in Lewes. Hoisting water samples onto the university's 125-foot research vessel, Dr. Sharp and Dr. Charles Culberson will then oversee analyses run by graduate students in the ship's innovative lab. Among current findings: The estuary is in relatively good condition and improving, probably the result of stricter controls on sewage disposal and industrial waste treatment.

Wrestled aboard miles out in the Atlantic Ocean, tuna (above) and other gamefish such as mackerel, blue marlin, and wahoo return with charter boats and private craft to marinas along Indian River Inlet. Smaller boats fish sea trout, flounder, and tautog from the sheltered waters of Indian River Bay.

Muscling a 30-pound bull rake, Rehoboth Bay clammer Bill Warther hoists a load of clams, oyster shells, and mud nearly double that weight into his 18-foot wooden skiff. Oysters were the bounty of this in-land bay before the parasite MSX struck in the 1950's. Now the oysters' remains shelter young clams that lodge in old oys-ter beds for anchorage and protection against predatory blue crabs.

A handful of young commercial clam-mers works the center of the bay year round. Summer tourists and local resi-dents comb the shallows for these clams, prized for their especially salty flavor.

An edible trophy of Atlantic tuna comes to dock at South Shore Marina on Indian River Inlet. Fishermen who release game fish and shark catches are encouraged to tag them for migration and behavior studies run by the National Marine Fisheries Service.

A vital new weapon in Delaware's war on mosquitoes, an amphibious rotary excavator plows ditches and creates ponds to give fish better access to mosquito-breeding areas. Research at the University of Delaware College of Marine Studies in Lewes shows that one fish species, the small killfish, can devour as many as 2,200 mosquito larvae a day. Using natural predators instead of insecticides has proven to be 99 percent effective in test areas. Unlike past digging machines, this excavator leaves no damaging mounds on the marsh—the peat it grinds is blown over the marsh in a fine slurry through which plants can quickly grow.

More than 2,000 miles of grid-pattern ditches were carved on Delaware's marshes between 1933 and 1938 when the Civilian Conservation Corps was enlisted to fight mosquitoes. Effective in draining mosquito breeding grounds, these ditches unfortunately also damaged the habitat of desirable wildlife. The state's Mosquito Control Section stopped maintenance of most straight-line ditches in the mid-1960's, but decades will pass before they grow over.

A dancer's agility surmounts all challenges at the annual Nanticoke Indian Powwow in Oak Orchard. Pressured by outsiders, most Nanticokes left Sussex County by the mid-18th century; the small number remaining have fought to keep their identity in a changing world. Delaware recognized the tribe in 1881 and today the Nanticoke Indian Association counts about 450 members. Proceeds from the Powwow have helped build the Nanticoke Museum.

In Delaware Seashore State Park (right), campers from Pennsylvania tuck into locally grown native American produce.

Venerable bald cypress trees stand sentinel in Trussum Pond as survivors of the Great Cypress Swamp—the northernmost natural cypress grove on the Atlantic Coast —lost over the centuries to timbering and farmland. Delaware Wild Lands now preserves the land around Trussum Pond and transplants cypress saplings on 11,000 acres of reclaimed swamp east of the pond.

A sentinel for mariners, the Inner Harbor Lighthouse in Lewes (above) stands on the Delaware Breakwater, built between 1829 and 1835 to deter shoaling. An outer breakwater called the Harbor of Refuge, the first of its kind in the Western Hemisphere, was completed in 1901. Both are now listed on the National Register of Historic Places.

Fishing on the wing, black skimmers
sweep over Rehoboth's Atlantic surf.

Bethany Beach lifeguards exchange signals above the throng on a summer weekend. The number of tourists from the Washington, D.C., and Baltimore areas began to soar after 1952 when the Chesapeake Bay Bridge cut travel time to the beach from a day to only a few hours.

Surf casting into the Atlantic from Delaware Seashore State Park yields seasonal catches of kingfish, bluefish, and sea trout. Even at the height of the summer season, surf fishers can work the park's lightly populated expanse, but most favor spring and fall, when the fish run strongest and crowds are lightest. Numerous tournaments from Fenwick Island to Cape Henlopen lure surf fishers to compete not only for the largest fish but also for the longest cast.

Wind and tide work their artistry on the sands in Cape Henlopen State Park, part of parkland owned by state and federal governments, that covers more than half of Delaware's 25-mile-long Atlantic coastline.

The Cape May-Lewes Ferry (left) made its first crossing between New Jersey and Delaware in 1964 and its growing fleet now carries more than 825,000 passengers annually. Bird watchers flock on deck in the fall and use the 17-mile-long trip across the mouth of Delaware Bay to spot migratory fowl. This Canadian tourist carries his bird with him.

Three cars is a full load when the Woodland Ferry (right) makes its 480-foot run across the Nanticoke River in southwest Sussex County. Operating from sunrise to sundown, the free ferry serves about 12,000 cars each year—not enough traffic to justify a bridge here, but ample business to sustain one of the nation's oldest ferry routes, established in 1793.

With the hush of evening, a sailboat becomes a private island for two in Lewes harbor.

"Patrolling with Rocky is as good as having an extra trooper in the car," says Delaware State Police canine officer Rich Ogden, watching officer Lloyd Massey run an exercise with his patrol partner, Ralph. Delaware's canine officers and their selected German shepherds train together as the dogs learn to track, attack, and sniff out explosives. "There's a great closeness between officer and dog," says Ogden. "We don't use cages in our cars, and you just have to get used to being licked on the ear."

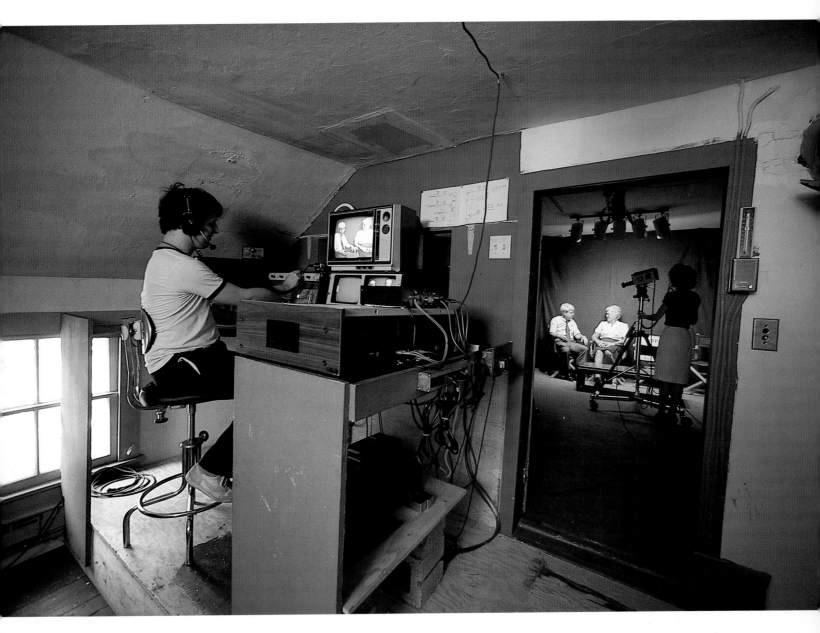

Delaware gained a second television station in 1981 when PBS affiliate WDPS began broadcasting from Seaford. Citizens seeking better television news coverage of southern Delaware organized to create this station. Lobbying in Washington, they made Delaware the first state to win cable deregulation so that downstate viewers can now legally receive a greater number of stations. The state's first television station, a branch of Philadelphia PBS affiliate WHYY, operates in Wilmington. No commercial stations are based in Delaware because it lies within the broadcasting range of Maryland and Philadelphia network affiliates.

A bumper crop of roadside markets sprouts across Sussex County each summer. At their fruit and vegetable stand near Georgetown, Ray and Sadie Thornton proudly offer a jumbo turban squash.

Ed Riggin tempts Rehoboth Beach traffic
with his recipe for a perennial summer
favorite.

"The signs aren't for sale," George Pass-
waters explains—several times a day—to
customers at Feedhouse Antiques near
Georgetown. "But we have to keep them
nailed down pretty good."

Waving the flag of the Diamond State, sailors push back to their boat after exploring an island in Rehoboth Bay. Tradition, if not historical evidence, holds that Thomas Jefferson bestowed on Delaware the nickname "a jewel of a state." Others speculate that the title Diamond State may be traced to Delaware poet John Lofland who, in 1847, aptly observed: "Delaware is like a diamond; diminutive, but having within it inherent value."

Beacon on Delaware's southern border, the Fenwick Island Lighthouse warned of shoals from 1859 to 1979. This barrier beach resort town then rallied to preserve it as a maritime monument. Boundary markers with the Calvert crest facing Maryland and the Penn crest facing Delaware were set in 1751 after this Transpeninsular Line was surveyed to the midpoint of the Delmarva Peninsula. From there, Mason and Dixon drew Delaware's western border to help resolve decades of legal boundary disputes.

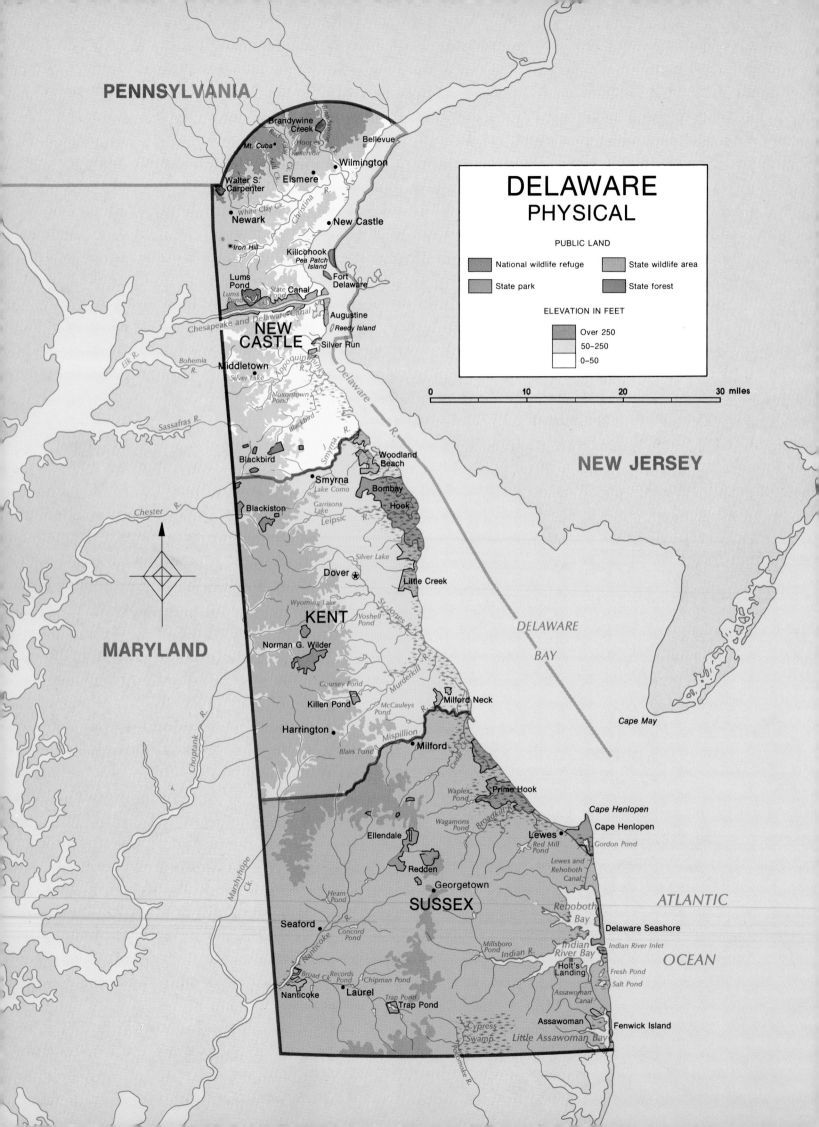

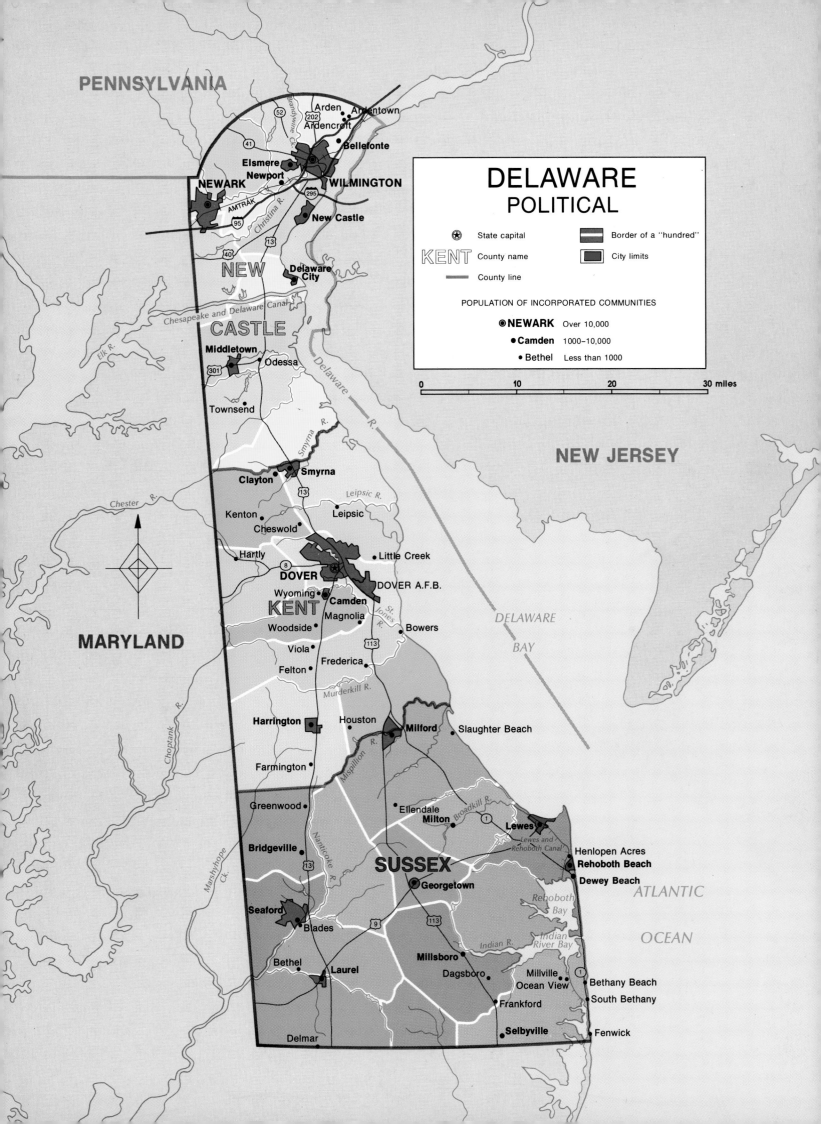

PENNSYLVANIA

Arden
Ardentown
52
202
Ardencroft
41
Bellefonte
Elsmere
Newport
NEWARK
WILMINGTON
295
AMTRAK
95
New Castle
Christina R.
13
40
NEW
Delaware
City

Chesapeake and Delaware Canal

CASTLE

Elk R.
Middletown
301
Odessa
Delaware R.
Townsend

Smyrna R.

NEW JERSEY

Chester R.
Clayton
Smyrna
13
Leipsic R.
Kenton
Leipsic
Cheswold
Hartly
Little Creek
8
DOVER
DOVER A.F.B.
Wyoming
St. Jones R.
KENT
Camden
Magnolia
DELAWARE
Woodside
Bowers
BAY
Viola
113
Felton
Frederica

Murderkill R.

MARYLAND

Choptank R.
Harrington
Houston
Milford
Slaughter Beach
Farmington

Mispillion R.

Greenwood
Ellendale
Broadkill R.
Milton
1
Lewes
Bridgeville
SUSSEX
Henlopen Acres
13
Rehoboth Beach
Georgetown
Dewey Beach
ATLANTIC
Seaford
Rehoboth
Bay
Blades
9
113
OCEAN
Bethel
Millsboro
Indian R.
Indian
River Bay
Laurel
Dagsboro
Millville
1
Ocean View
Bethany Beach
Frankford
South Bethany
Selbyville
Fenwick
Delmar

Nanticoke R.
Marshyhope Ck.

DELAWARE
POLITICAL

⍟ State capital
KENT County name
County line

▬ Border of a "hundred"
■ City limits

POPULATION OF INCORPORATED COMMUNITIES

◉ NEWARK Over 10,000
● Camden 1000–10,000
• Bethel Less than 1000

0   10   20   30 miles

Kevin Fleming: Photographer

Delaware-born Kevin Fleming has circled the globe as a photographer for *National Geographic* magazine since 1979. His assignments have carried him from war and famine in East Africa to the Mediterranean, Florida, and the complex world of high energy physics. Covering the Sinai Peninsula in 1981, he was caught in the crossfire when assassins felled Egypt's President Anwar Sadat. Fleming escaped with his life—and some of the few photographs of that tragedy, later published by *Newsweek* and more than a dozen international magazines. He was honored that year as runner-up Magazine Photographer of the Year by the National Press Photographers Association.

Fleming began his career at the *Delaware State News* in Dover in 1972 after attending Wesley College. Two years later he joined the photography staff of the *News-Journal* in Wilmington and was three times named Pennsylvania Press Photographer of the Year. In 1983, for a *National Geographic* article on Delaware, he again looked homeward, focusing his camera on his native state, an assignment that led to the expanded coverage in this book. Fleming still roves the world but he now lives in Annapolis, Maryland.

Carol E. Hoffecker: Introduction

A native of Delaware, Carol E. Hoffecker is Richards Professor and Chairperson of the Department of History at the University of Delaware. A graduate of the University of Delaware, she earned a Ph.D. in American History at Harvard University in 1967. Hoffecker is the author of a number of publications dealing with state, local, and urban history, including *Wilmington, Delaware: Portrait of An Industrial City* (University of Virginia Press, 1974), *Delaware, A Bicentennial History* (Norton, 1977), *Wilmington: A Pictorial History* (Donning, 1982), and *Corporate Capital: Wilmington In The Twentieth Century* (Temple University Press). In addition to her writing, Carol Hoffecker is well known throughout Delaware as a speaker on historical subjects.

Jane Vessels:
Text

Born in Oklahoma and raised in Miami, Florida, Jane Vessels joined the staff of *National Geographic* magazine after graduating from Duke University in 1977. Specializing in picture text, she has written about such diverse topics as armadillos, Ireland, Papua New Guinea, potatoes, and the restoration of Leonardo da Vinci's "Last Supper"—and now *Delaware, Small Wonder.*

Marley E. Amstutz:
Maps

Born and raised in California, Marley Amstutz took his degree in Geography at University of California, Davis and his master's degree at University of Kansas. Continuing his eastward trek across the map of the United States, he began working in Delaware in 1980 as a cartographer for Eleutherian Mills-Hagley Foundation (Hagley Museum).

Amstutz's maps have been published in books by the Foundation, Temple University Press, Johns Hopkins University Press, Saunders Publishing Company, and in numerous periodicals.

Married and the father of a young son, he is currently living and working as a cartographer in Lancaster, Pennsylvania.

The Dedication,
Introduction, and captions
for this book were set in
12 point, 11½ point, and 9 point
Melior (592 medium), respectively.
The face was designed by
Herman Zapf for D. Stempel AG
who issued the face in 1952.
The display type was set in varying
sizes of Helvetica (500 light).
The face was designed
by M. Miedinger for Haas of
Switzerland who issued the face
in 1957. All type was set by
U.S. Lithograph Inc.,
New York.

The paper for this
book is Top-Coated 157 gram.
The book was printed and
bound by Dai Nippon Printing
Company, Ltd., Tokyo,
Japan.

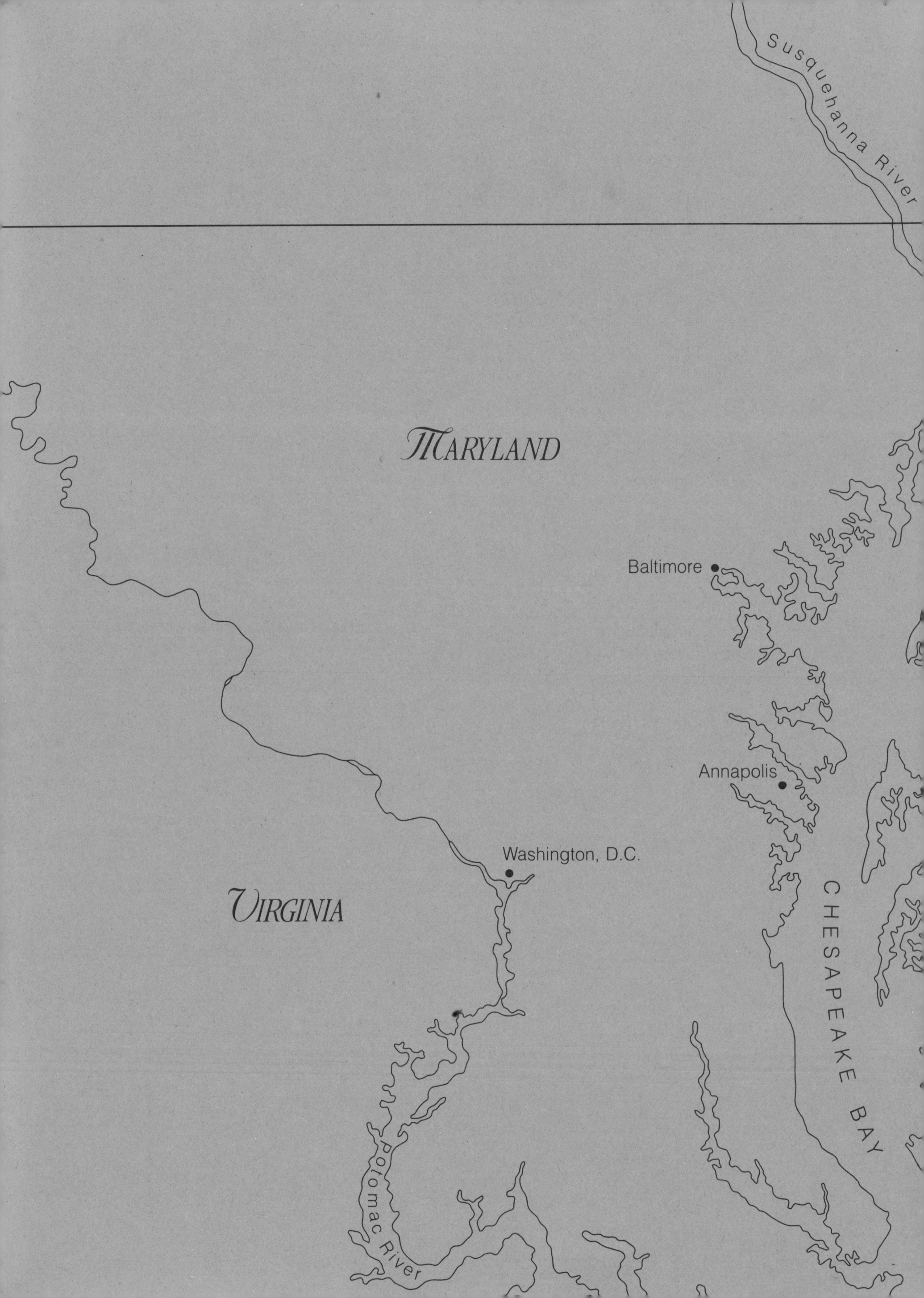
Susquehanna River
MARYLAND
Baltimore
Annapolis
Washington, D.C.
VIRGINIA
CHESAPEAKE BAY
Potomac River